Praise for *Terrorists on the Border and in Our County*

"Throughout this important book, Charles A. Marino methodically details the impact of the Biden administration's decisions to dismantle effective policies and abandon their federal responsibility of providing national security for the American people. Marino lends his decades of experience to the readers in not only identifying the causes of the current border crisis but also in charting a practical path forward."

—MARK MORGAN, Visiting Fellow, Border Security and Immigration Center, Heritage Foundation

TERRORISTS ON THE BORDER AND IN OUR COUNTRY

TERRORISTS ON THE BORDER AND IN OUR COUNTRY

CHARLES A. MARINO

Humanix Books

www.humanixbooks.com

*To the brave yet underappreciated patriots on the front lines,
tirelessly protecting our homeland each and every day.*

Contents

Foreword

As the former Acting Commissioner of Customs and Border Protection (CBP) under the Trump administration and Chief of the U.S. Border Patrol under the Obama administration, I understand how vital it is to secure our borders against a vast set of complex threats that jeopardize our safety and national security.

The unmitigated chaos occurring along our borders under the Biden administration has been the result of reckless political- and ideological-driven policies that place America last.

As the chief architect of these policies, Secretary Alejandros Mayorkas dismantled the effective network of tools, authorities, and policies we had in place, and has, in effect, handed operational control of our borders to the Mexican cartels.

The historic level of illegal immigration, human trafficking, drugs, and national security threats pouring across our borders during the past three years clearly illustrate that our policies worked. They also signaled to the CBP and U.S. Immigration and Customs Enforcement (ICE) workforce that we stood with them through all challenges while telling the rest of the world that *legal* immigration was the only acceptable way into the greatest nation on the planet!

Throughout this important book, Charles Marino methodically details the impact of the Biden administration's decisions to dismantle effective policies and abandon their federal responsibility of providing national security for the American people. Marino lends his decades of experience to the readers in not only identifying the causes of the current border crisis but also in charting a practical path forward.

Mark Morgan
Visiting Fellow, Border Security
and Immigration Center
Heritage Foundation

Author's Note

As a national security executive, father, and proud American, I have always cared deeply about the security of the United States and the protection of American families. I believe this to be the number one priority of any president of the United States, Republican or Democrat. It is why as a young Secret Service agent I swore an oath to not only protect our country from enemies both foreign and domestic, but to also provide sound security advice to the leader of the free world regardless of their party affiliation. I believe that a person in my position and with my experience must cast politics aside and call it as it is. Failing to do so is a disservice to all Americans and one that could ultimately lead to our great nation's demise. A country is not sovereign or safe without securing its borders and enforcing immigration laws. This is an indisputable fact! These two essential pillars are necessary to protect the homeland of any country. They are not unique to the United States. For anyone to think otherwise is foolish at best—treasonish at worst—which is why most countries around the world make enforcing them a priority. It's what I and many other U.S. national security experts call a no-brainer. Yet 22 years after the terrorist attacks on September

11, 2001, the United States finds itself in a national security crisis because of a president and administration who have placed politics over national security, leaving border states scrambling to protect citizens the best they can, often in defiance of the federal government.

It is personally heartbreaking that the policies of the Biden administration have made the country less safe since 9/11 by directly undercutting the very purpose for creating the Department of Homeland Security under the 2002 Homeland Security Act, and by subverting the statutory responsibilities of the Border Patrol, ICE, and practically every other agency tasked with protecting the homeland. In just three years in office, the Biden Administration has fundamentally changed the face of America, to be sure. The consequences of letting 10 million or more illegal immigrants into the country in such a short amount of time will be realized in the years to come. We must try our best to fix the problem right now; then we must hope it's not too late.

Before we can fix any large-scale problem, we must first identify exactly what created it. That's what this book does. Then it offers solutions. Readers will learn the role politics—the unquenchable thirst for power—play in national security decisions. We must come to understand that when it comes to the security of the country, the final decisions made by elected leaders are not always in the best interest of Americans.

Thank you for purchasing this book. It gives me faith that you are just as concerned about the future of our glorious country as I am. Now, together, we must act.

Introduction

We are not saying, "Don't come." We are saying, "Don't come now . . . ."

> —With these calculated words from
> DHS Secretary Alejandro Mayorkas during
> an official White House Press Corps address on
> March 1, 2021, the message was sent to the world that
> America's southwest border would soon be wide open
> to anyone wishing to enter.

Fifteen-year-old Maria and her tightly knit family heard the news from small-town gossip and on social media: Incoming U.S. President Joe Biden promised to stop construction of Trump's border wall immediately upon taking office and to offer refuge to anyone who could reach American soil under a simple verbal claim of "asylum." For millions of desperate folks from impoverished areas all over the world, this new messaging was an invitation—a welcome mat—compared to Trump's policies that required immigrants to stay in Mexico while their individual cases were investigated.

Word on the streets of Chihuahua suggested that if Maria could just make it across the border, she'd be free to make a life in America. Her cousins, who had legally immigrated to California in 2005, urged her to come, insisting there'd be plenty of jobs available when she arrived. Getting there, however, would be on her.

As an "unaccompanied child," she had been told she had little to worry about. She also had heard that even if she were to be apprehended by U.S. authorities, her journey might simply be delayed for a few days as she was processed and released for a court hearing sometime in the years to come. And if, for any reason, she were to be expelled back to Mexico, under America's new COVID rules, there would be no penalties for trying again. For Maria, the odds were worth the risk. But as always, there was the money issue.

She had lost her father to a motorcycle accident when she was 13 and had to drop out of school to help her mother feed her brother and sisters. They figured if she could make it to California, where the poor are given housing, food, and health-care, she could send money home and eventually bring the whole family to live with her.

So, finally, with the help of small donations from extended family and some street wisdom garnered from two tough years of fending for herself, Maria felt she was ready. She Snapchatted an acquaintance, who made a few calls. A week later, she hopped a ride to a tiny town outside of Ciudad Juárez, where she met up with a coyote who promised to usher her across the border.

As soon as she saw him, Maria knew she'd made a mistake.

His body was laden with wicked tattoos—one that she vividly remembered depicted a bloody cross and a dead dove underneath it. When he turned, she saw the flash of a hand-gun partially hidden in his waistband. She noticed its grip was wrapped in silvery duct tape. He looked her up and down like a meat inspector before sneering in approval. Maria's natural beauty was both a blessing and a curse. The coyote's wicked smile vanished as he demanded the money.

Maria was already in too deep; she had no choice but to reach into her bag to fish out her life savings—U.S. $2,000—knowing that she must pay the remaining balance of her bill within three months after reaching the States and that she would likely be forced to work for the cartels for even longer, once in the country. What that "job" would entail was unknown.

From the moment she handed him the cash and was shoved into a Ford pickup, she was not treated like a client paying for a service but rather like a stock animal headed to auction. She was pleasantly surprised, though, when her trip across the Rio Grande was much less treacherous than the drowning nightmare she had anticipated; minutes later, when she felt American soil under her feet, she started to relax a bit. But her easiness was short-lived. For another five tortuous months, Maria would not taste the American freedom that she'd dreamed of. Rather, her nightmare was just beginning.

As soon as she changed into dry clothes pulled from the only luggage she carried—a plastic bag—she was ushered up a steep riverbank, led across a few hundred yards of crop fields and finally onto a culvert beside a dirt road where they hid. An hour or so later, another pickup appeared. She was ordered to lay down in its covered bed and not to move. Lying beside her were several plastic containers filled with packaged cocaine— and as she would later learn—enough fentanyl to kill most of Dallas.

Maria was driven for six suffocating hours west on U.S. Highway 10 before the truck made its first and only stop. She thanked God that it was a relatively cool morning in October, or she surely would have baked to death. But before she could discern any of her new surroundings, she was blindfolded and whisked into a seedy, windowless bedroom in a stash house somewhere in Tucson. She was pushed to a bed, given a sack of fast food and some Xanax pills, and told she needed to rest awhile before continuing her journey to California and her new life.

But there would be no journey. For months on end the young girl's life was a haze of violence, drugs, sleep, and rape.

Maria was sold into prostitution and used by cartel members—day after day, night after night. Like every kidnapping story you've ever heard, she was told that if she were to try to run, therefore defaulting on her debt, she would be tortured, and her mother and little brother back in Chihuahua would be killed. And she had every reason to believe her captors, as she'd witnessed their savagery on numerous occasions and overheard many of the vile deeds they'd done while they partied in the next room and bragged about their gang-banging exploits, including intentionally killing "stupid American teenagers" by selling them fentanyl-laced cocaine. So Maria entered survival mode, doing what she had to do to live, trying to block out all the rest, all while praying for an opportunity to escape her living hell— whenever she was lucid enough to do so.

Despite Maria's life-altering physical and mental scars, she's among the lucky; a raid on the stash house, thanks to an informant's tip, landed her in the custody of the U.S. Drug

Enforcement Administration (DEA), who promptly turned her over to ICE. Her whereabouts to this day are confidential.

———————

As Americans, we all hope Maria is safe and somehow prospering, wherever she is. But the problem of illegal immigration on a mass scale is only getting worse, and it will continue to do so until America's border and immigration laws are enforced and its messaging to illegal immigrants serves as a deterrent, not an invitation. What we do know for sure is that, despite what President Biden's incompetent and absentee "Border Czar," Vice President Kamala Harris, attempts to spin, the border is, most definitely, *not* secure. It's an insult to the American peoples' intelligence to suggest otherwise.

Sickeningly, Maria's story isn't unique. Tens of thousands—possibly hundreds of thousands—like hers have occurred since this crisis started. And human trafficking is just one horrific by-product of America's leaders losing operational control of our border. Others sneak into America not for a better life or even for a more lucrative one selling illicit drugs and guns to its vast and wealthy markets. Rather, professionally trained terrorists come specifically to destroy it via bombs. At the time of this writing, news of the thousands of Chinese, Iranian, and Russian nationals being caught at the southern border—some of them suspected of being foreign agents, while others are on the terrorist watch list—is commonplace. Meanwhile, Central American–style gangs, like the notorious MS-13, continue to fuel their ruthless criminal enterprises in American cities via drugs, theft, kidnapping, extortion, and murder. On a less-violent note, even well-intended illegal immigrants take jobs that could be filled by legal immigrants and U.S. citizens alike, all while not paying back into the system via income taxes but rather fleecing it by sending their earnings home or satisfying their remaining debt owed to the cartels.

America's resources and infrastructure, such as its welfare systems, housing, hospitals, schools, and police departments, are all stretched like pawnshop guitar strings, while once-great American cities from coast to coast are morphing into virtual border towns before our very eyes. Still, elite, progressive leftists maintain that America is incorrigibly racist and should be ashamed of itself for not letting everyone in.

President Biden and his administration claim that their open-border politics are borne of empathy for the world's impoverished peoples. But where is that same empathy for lower- and middle-class Americans, who bear the brunt of unfettered illegal immigration? Biden's reluctance to enforce the border and immigration laws of the United States demonstrates that abandoning his sworn federal responsibilities has done nothing but endanger the lives of immigrants and citizens alike, making the country a more dangerous place for everyone.

While illegal immigrants are receiving free plane tickets, hotel stays, meals, smartphones, and healthcare, you might be surprised how many poor kids in rural Oklahoma trailer parks don't have toothpaste or access to medicine, much less a decent education or a half-ass chance at success. Yet, we seldom if ever hear this administration talk about helping them. Sioux Nation members on the Rosebud Reservation in South Dakota have one of the highest poverty rates this country has witnessed since the Great Depression, and the substance-abuse and unemployment rates are off the charts, but you seldom hear about these issues, because they're a progressive embarrassment and because the Rosebud Sioux are treated as a federally recognized nation, so its statistics needn't be reported as U.S. statistics. So the media and lawmakers conveniently sweep them under the rug, all to continue the narrative they want to push.

As of late 2023, major cities within the country mimic the scenes of a horror movie; Chicago averages 60 murders per month, and Los Angeles homeless situation is untenable. San Francisco boasts of its sanctuary status, but it's a real-life Gotham City with its "defund the police" movement that provides sanctuary only for criminals as they steal, loot, pillage, defecate in public, and get high at will as business owners flee. New York City is pure mayhem as its liberal mayor begs the federal government for relief.

Yet each day, the news shows more immigrants spilling into the country from our southern border, unvetted, as tax-paying Americans can only watch and wonder how many more resources and opportunities their country can hand out. Others, somehow, think we haven't handed out enough.

But before we delve fully into America's immigration crisis, which has swiftly become a national security crisis, all of us must know that "refugee" and "asylee," as official U.S. immigration law defines them, do not mean "an escape from poverty" or "a wish to live a better life in America." According to Title 8, Section 1101(A)(42):

The term "refugee" means (A) any person who is outside any country of such person's nationality or, in the case of a person having no nationality, is outside any country in which such person last habitually resided, and who is unable or unwilling to return to, and is unable or unwilling to avail himself or herself of the protection of, that country because of persecution or a well-founded fear of persecution on account of race, religion, nationality, membership in a particular social group, or political opinion.

An "asylee," or "asylum seeker" as you will read often in the pages ahead, according to the Department of Homeland Security (DHS) official website is "… a person who meets the definition of refugee and is already present in the United States or is seeking admission at a port of entry."

Sadly, there are billions of innocent people around the globe suffering from abject poverty. As much as we wish we could, we can't possibly save them all. We must steel ourselves to this definition—the law—as we move forward.

Here's another fact we must remember: A country cannot be considered sovereign, or safe, without secure borders. The leaders of every prosperous nation in the history of the world have known this, perhaps with the strange exception of the Biden administration and the radical leftists in Congress at the universities, and in the media.

As of 2023, America's political divide combined with foolish policies have created a perfect storm, and if we don't circle the wagons now—specifically at the polling booths in 2024—our nation's days of prosperity—the very reason people by the millions risk their lives to come to America—will come to an end. Its current trajectory simply cannot be sustained.

Before we can fully delve into border security, immigration policy, and how to fix these problems, though, we should first take a truncated and unbiased look at the United States and Mexico's relatively brief history as neighbors and the policies that have resulted. After all, to ignore history is to invite ignorance into future planning.

America-Mexico Border Policy Timeline

1819. The Adams-Onis Treaty between Spain and the United States defines the border between Spanish property (now Mexico) and America's Louisiana Territory.

1821. Mexico wins independence from Spain, and the border between Mexico and the United States becomes the southern boundary of the newly formed Mexican Republic.

1830. Mexico bans immigration from the United States to rid its lands of English-speaking people.

1836. The Republic of Texas declares independence from Mexico, leading to the establishment of a disputed border between Texas and Mexico.

1845. The United States annexes Texas, further escalating tensions over the border.

1846–1848. The Mexican-American War results in the Treaty of Guadalupe Hidalgo. The treaty establishes the Rio Grande as the boundary between Mexico and the United States, with the United States acquiring vast territories, including present-day California, Nevada, Utah, Arizona, New Mexico, and parts of Colorado and Wyoming.

1853. The Gadsden Purchase is made for $10 million, buying the United States additional land from Mexico for the construction of a southern transcontinental railroad. This purchase further solidifies the United States–Mexico border.

1882. The Chinese Exclusion Act is passed, marking the first federal law that restricts immigration into the United States. Border inspection stations are erected.

1904. Agents are assigned to patrol the border to better enforce the Chinese Exclusion Act.

1910–1920. The Mexican Revolution takes place, leading to increased migration from Mexico to the United States, primarily driven by economic and political instability.

1924. The Immigration Act of 1924 (the Johnson-Reed Act) establishes a quota system for immigration, setting annual limits based on nationality and requiring fees for visas. It restricts immigration from Mexico. The U.S. Border Patrol is officially established.

1942. The Bracero Program is implemented, allowing temporary agricultural laborers from Mexico to work in the United States to address labor shortages during World War II and its aftermath.

1944. Title 42 (federal law) is crafted to prevent the spread of communicable diseases. It allowed the United States to swiftly deny migrants and/or asylum seekers entry if there were a national health crisis, pandemic, or other outbreak, such as tuberculosis. Title 42, Section 265 states:

> *Whenever the Surgeon General determines that by reason of the existence of any communicable disease in a foreign country there is serious danger of the introduction of such*

disease into the United States, and that this danger is so increased by the introduction of persons or property from such country that a suspension of the right to introduce such persons and property is required in the interest of the public health, the Surgeon General, in accordance with regulations approved by the President, shall have the power to prohibit, in whole or in part, the introduction of persons and property from such countries or places as he shall designate in order to avert such danger, and for such period of time as he may deem necessary for such purpose.

Likely because violators of Title 42 were instantly repelled from crossing the border and not arrested and tried, it imposed no penalty on migrants for trying to cross the border illegally, as Title 8 does today.

1947. The United States and Mexico ratify the Inter-American Treaty of Reciprocal Assistance, which provides that an attack on one nation is to be considered an attack upon the others. (The United States would later evoke the "Rio Act" after the terrorist attacks of 9/11.)

1954. Operation Wetback employs the U.S. military to detain and deport illegal immigrants. The policy was quietly encouraged by the Mexican government, which believed that Mexico was losing too many laborers to the United States.

1965. The Immigration and Nationality Act abolishes the national-origins quota system and establishes a preference-based system focusing on family reunification and skilled labor. It results in increased immigration from Mexico and other parts of the world.

1969. The War on Drugs officially begins. The United States installs agents on the border to inspect all materials and persons attempting to enter the country for illegal narcotics.

1973. The U.S. Drug Enforcement Administration (DEA) is established.

1980. Congress passes Title 8 of the U.S. Code of Federal Regulations, which establishes official immigration laws and defines "aliens." According to U.S. Code (Title 8, Section 215.1 Definitions (A): "The term *alien* means any person who is not a citizen or national of the United States."

1986. The Immigration Reform and Control Act (IRCA) is enacted, granting amnesty to certain undocumented immigrants who entered the United States prior to 1982. It implements penalties for employers who knowingly hire undocumented workers.

1994. The North American Free Trade Agreement (NAFTA) is signed to promote an economic partnership among the United States, Mexico, and Canada.

2001. In the aftermath of the September 11 attacks, the U.S. government strengthens border security measures and creates the Department of Homeland Security (DHS) to bolster border and national security. As of 2023, the monstrous DHS consists of 260,000 employees across 26 divisions, including Customs and Border Protection (CBP), Coast Guard, U.S. Citizenship and Immigration Services, Federal Emergency Management Agency (FEMA), Federal Law Enforcement Training Center, Immigrations and Customs Enforcement (ICE), U.S. Secret Service, Transportation Security Administration (TSA), Office of Intelligence and Analysis, Countering Weapons of Mass Destruction, and others. It should be noted that the U.S. Border Patrol is a subdivision of the CBP, although CBP agents and Border Patrol agents are responsible for differing tasks.

2006. The Secure Fence Act is signed into law, authorizing the construction of physical barriers along the United States–Mexico border.

2008. The Mérida Initiative antidrug/anticartel plan is launched. The United States provides Mexico with weapons, intelligence, training, technology, aircraft, and funds to combat importation of illegal drugs and the crime that comes with them. Significantly, the language of the agreement between the United States and Mexico used the phrase "shared responsibility," signifying that the leaders of both countries wished to work together to solve a mutual problem. The plan budgeted more than $500 million annually over three years.

2012. The Deferred Action for Childhood Arrivals (DACA) program is introduced by executive action. It is designed to provide temporary relief from deportation for certain undocumented immigrants who arrived in the United States as minors.

2013. Mérida 2.0 is launched. It renewed the 2008 agreement between the United States and Mexico to work together in trying to combat the proliferation of drugs and cartel violence in both countries. President Obama's version outlined four pillars of focus, including disrupting criminal organizations, institutionalizing the rule of law, building a twenty-first century border, and building strong and resilient community. However, judging by the budgets appropriated to each pillar, Obama shifted Mérida 2.0's priority from law enforcement and border security to criminal justice reform.

2015. Nearly 700 miles of border fence are completed.

2016. Newly elected U.S. President Donald Trump promises to build a border wall.

2018. Due to an immigration surge largely spurred by the collapse of Central American economies, U.S. President Donald Trump launches the Migrant Protection Protocols (MPP) initiative (also called "Remain in Mexico"), which forces asylum seekers who immigrate via Mexico to wait out their probationary period in Mexico rather than in the United States.

2020. The United States, Mexico, and Canada sign the United States–Mexico–Canada (USMCA) agreement, essentially NAFTA 2.0. Mexico passes a law that requires any Mexican official to get approval from a Mexican panel before meeting with U.S. agents. The law effectively cools drug enforcement relations between the two countries in that due to Mexican corruption, any such discussions or panel approval would likely compromise sensitive intelligence and put American agents at risk. Title 42 is evoked by President Trump; it allows the United States to quickly turn immigrants and asylum seekers away at the border due to COVID-19 fears.

2021. President Joe Biden takes office and signs several executive actions to reverse Trump-era immigration policies. The construction of the border wall is halted. Biden reverses Trump's "Remain in Mexico" policy; he is initially overruled by the courts, but ultimately succeeds in reversing it. The southern border is reopened after COVID-19 fears subside.

2022. Migration at the border spikes to a then-all-time high in May of 2022, when the United States apprehends 239,416 illegal immigrants in one month as they try to cross the border.

May 2023. Title 42 is lifted under Biden; in the three years prior, it was used more than 2.8 million times to deny asylum seekers entry. The immigration code reverts to Title 8. Asylum seekers are now processed on U.S. soil, and an estimated 85 percent are allowed entry. The Biden administration announces it will grant temporary protected status and work permits for roughly 500,000 Venezuelans who were in the country prior to July 31. DEA reports 73,400,000 fentanyl pills have been seized in 2023.

June 2023. Secretary Alejandro Mayorkas issues orders to reinstate its so-called Sanctuary Country initiative, which forbids ICE agents from arresting and deporting illegal aliens that have not been recently convicted of violent crimes. He announces that ". . . the majority of undocumented noncitizens . . . are not priorities for removal."

October 1, 2023. Illegal immigration spikes again. The end of September witnesses over 10,000 illegal immigrants per day crossing the border from Mexico into the United States. Texas Governor Greg Abbott declares an invasion and sends in Texas National Guard troops to help secure the border in Eagle Pass, Texas, where they are met with resistance from federal troops sent by Biden who are photographed by news sources cutting the border fence to help illegal immigrants cross the border.

October 30. Judge Alia Moses of the U.S. District Court for the Western District of Texas orders the DHS to cease "disassembling, degrading, tampering" miles of fence running along the border.

2024. Time will tell.

TERRORISTS ON THE BORDER AND IN OUR COUNTRY

CHAPTER ONE

Strong Borders: Vital for Security and Sovereignty

It is a fundamental right and duty for a nation to protect the integrity of its borders and its laws. This Administration shall stand firm against illegal immigration and the continued abuse of our immigration laws. By closing the back door to illegal immigration, we will continue to open the front door to legal immigrants.

—President Bill Clinton, Memorandum of President of the United States, February 7, 1995, 60 F.R. 7885

The United States–Mexico border: A geopolitical divide covering 1,954 miles over desert sand, water, cities, towns, public lands, and private property alike; an average of 350 million documented humans traverse it per year, making it the most heavily crossed border on Earth. As of 2023, it's also the most dangerous overland border crossing on Earth.

For all but the most ideologically and emotionally driven people, listing the reasons why borders are vital for America's national security, sovereignty, and independence is asinine. Neither America nor any other nation would be recognized as a nation if it had no borders.

If you're reading this, you already know why.

But because a portion of this book is meant to be used as a guide for countering arguments from radicals who relish anarchy in America's streets and dismembering her institutions until she is no longer recognizable, please humor me as I list just a few of the primary reasons for establishing, maintaining, and protecting America's borders.

For starters, borders define the territorial extent of a nation and help create a distinct national identity, which includes shared cultural values, traditions, language, history, camaraderie, and a legal system. Opponents of strong borders cite these things as being detrimental—racist, even—to the "melting pot of cultures" and languages that America is. But can anyone imagine an America where people were not encouraged to assimilate into its culture or mandated to follow laws passed by democratic processes, or even attempt to speak a common language? There's little doubt that the myriad tribal groups that would certainly spring up and lay claim to their chosen corner of the country would mix like oil and water if they couldn't communicate, understand each other's needs, or even heed basic traffic laws that prevent daily carnage. Can you imagine over 350 million people of 195 various nations attempting to get along with nothing but the innate human will for survival in common? Even the Left's darlings—Bill Clinton and Barack Obama—realized that peoples of a unified country must have some things in common, such as language and laws, if it is to have any national identity at all. Both said as much in speeches during their terms in office.

Without clearly demarcated and enforced geographical borders, America couldn't enact its social systems, including welfare, social security, tax codes, or the copious affirmative action laws the Left so dearly loves. Why not welfare systems? If you ever tried to give out free lemonade in a busy neighborhood when you were a child—thinking you'd do something kind—you likely learned an eye-opening lesson: There's never enough lemonade for everyone. Likewise, if everyone were allowed to cross the borders at will to freely accept America's handouts, there'd soon be no more welfare left to give. America's taxpayers, footing the bill for all comers, would ultimately go broke, thereby lowering everyone's standard of living. It's happened time after time in socialist countries throughout world history, and in fact it's happening now in cities such as Chicago and New York where immigrants are arriving only to realize the milk and honey have already been handed out. And as we are seeing now as inflation soars and our national debt pushes us near the point of default, printing more money is not a viable option. Indeed, America is on the brink.

Moreover, those who bemoan America's "unfair" immigration policies are often the same people who cry for more taxes—more money to be redistributed among the people. But with no borders, those who enter the country illegally aren't documented, and therefore they cannot be easily taxed, except for sales tax if they choose to spend their dollars stateside. (Perhaps this is one point that both American political factions might agree on—taxation—and one that should be explored in political debates to come.) As it stands now, American taxpayers are handing out billions to *fund* illegal immigration but getting little to nothing in return except more crime and less security. This must change if America is to continue her exceptional, though relatively short, run of prosperity.

The unfortunate reality is planet Earth is a rock rotating in space that contains finite livable land and resources, as is the fantastic experiment in self-government that is America. This fact is obvious to most of us, but these days it bears reminding that America's border security—along with national censuses, sound immigration policy, and law enforcement—allows us to better manage how many people can immigrate to America, for the benefit of all Americans as well as millions of fortunate immigrants. To date, America is home to 45 million documented immigrants. It's only been in very recent years—a blip in human history—that a faction of utopian-dreaming "globalists" seem to believe that if there were no borders on Earth, everyone would simply get along, with an equal number of people voluntarily living in the high-mountain deserts of Afghanistan or atop the Siberian tundra, while others would naturally feel more at home lounging on the 75-degree beaches of San Diego or Miami. Unfortunately, human nature isn't programmed that way. We all desire easy living. And Americans are among the world's luckiest for being born winners of the geographical lottery. Most of us don't take it for granted.

Utopia doesn't exist on Earth and never will. It's a noble idea but a naive one typically reserved for spoiled college students fresh after finishing Karl Marx's manifesto. They're dancing with 10 of their like-minded friends and feeling quite sure that if they could all get along so swimmingly while sharing a joint and listening to Rage Against the Machine, why couldn't *everyone* in the world? Normally, the notion passes as the THC wears off, or for others, with wisdom gained through real-world experience.

But more frequently these days, as Gen-Zers languish in their parents' basements affixed to the household insurance policy and TikTok, the dream becomes an obsession. At some point, after being whipped into a frenzy by the news media's incessant reports of America's corporations destroying the entire Earth, and proclamations that white supremacy is the number one threat to national security, some fall into a self-righteous mania that rationalizes destroying property, dismantling proven American institutions such as free speech, trying to erase history, and even committing overt acts of violence against others who do not share the same views.

In the past, these notions were a normal part of the coming-of-age process. The difference now is they have been normalized by the liberal elite to the point that a large swath of American society believes that being proud of America is somehow offensive to people of other nations. So, they try to dismantle the parts of America they do not agree with, even if it means breaking the law to do it. Others simply seem to loathe mankind in general, believing the planet would be better off without us.

The fact is, no civilized society has survived without law and order. Without it, societies will inevitably collapse. Perhaps this is what they want.

The cold, hard truth is this: Throughout human history, wars—not hugs—have shaped the world's borders. To deny this flaw of humanity is to leave your prosperity vulnerable to those who are waiting outside the gates, licking their chops for an opportunity to snatch it. Borders help keep the wolves at bay. They also help regulate, conserve, and distribute a nation's limited resources; a nation can either vigorously defend them or risk being annexed into the domain of the next empire. It's happened again and again throughout human history, and it's seldom accomplished by nonviolent means. And if it happens, there's a good chance we won't adore the worldviews and social systems of our conquerors, and they likely won't care for ours.

Historically, when people invade other peoples' territory, war breaks out. There should be a war right now, 2023, at America's southern border, because we are being criminally invaded. Puzzlingly, to all prideful Americans, however, our current leaders are not repelling the invasion but aiding it. I'm talking about Democrats *and* Republicans.

Our country is our castle, and its borders are our moat—the physical manifestation of the proverbial line in the sand that warns would-be enemies that if they cross it, they must be willing to pay the consequences. Our moat has a name. It's called the Rio Grande. It must be guarded and always reinforced.

"Son," my father once told me when I suggested we tear down our backyard fence so my neighborhood buddies and I could combine all the yards to make a regulation-size football field, "the neighbors are great. But let's keep the fence so the Johnsons' Rottweiler doesn't come in here and kill us." Pop was wise.

As a realist who's spent time in many other parts of the world implementing strategies of security on a large scale, I'm all too aware of the evil that exists in this world. By *evil*, I don't mean witchcraft but rather the otherwise ordinary people who will rob, kill, or displace others if doing so could benefit them. Whether born of desperate economic conditions, religious beliefs, no parental guidance, or pure psychopathy, it matters not; evil has existed since the dawn of man, violence has been around since the lion was made to eat the impala, and it will continue forevermore. Nowadays, however, it seems too easy for pampered, inexperienced, and ideologically driven Americans to believe that all peoples of less fortunate countries are naturally nice.

As much as I'd love to believe it, too, rest assured it is not the case: America as we know it would have ceased to exist soon after it was established if it hadn't been for her borders that were vigorously defended with bullets, blades, and bloodshed at all costs; first from Santa Anna's assault on the Alamo, then internally during the Civil War, then from Japan and Germany in World War II and countless other threats that were extinguished by our proud military without much fanfare. You can bet your last U.S.-minted silver dollar that if not for our customs agents and intelligence officers and their vigorous defense at every international airport in America, today there would be endless versions of 9/11; indeed, many of our cities and national monuments would be piles of rubble if all visitors were allowed unfettered access to our shores.

Trust me when I tell you that there are millions of people in this world who hate America for its freedoms and who will not relent in their quest to rid the world of America, Americans, and all for which they stand—including our freedom of religion, free speech, women's rights, minority rights, universal suffrage, alcohol use, abortion, LGBTQ rights, pot smoking, and nearly every other right that Americans so dearly defend. Others are simply envious of what we have and want it for themselves.

Certainly, most immigrants simply want a better life for themselves and their families. Few blame them for wanting a piece of the promised land, and if the situations were reversed, I might well do the same. But by the same token, I wouldn't blame them for defending their homeland either, just as they shouldn't blame me for wanting the best possible lives for my children and all American children who live under a vast umbrella of common values. Other governments of the world have no qualms about defending their values. Why shouldn't we?

Some ivory tower Americans seem to forget that all prosperous countries have strong border policies. Have you ever tried to enter Canada? If you have had a DUI on your record from a regrettable night while in college—a record that the United States shares with Canada—there's a good chance that you'll be denied entry for your vacation! Wish to immigrate to China? Good luck! If you don't have direct family there, the only other pathway is to apply as an investor. All you need is a minimum of $500,000 ($2,000,000 works better) and bona fide tax records to prove you invested it in communist China! Poland is proud of the fact that it has the lowest crime rate in Europe and has had zero terrorist acts in many years. It's also proud of its culture and openly boasts that it will permit no Muslims to enter. When asked by Cathy Newman of England's Channel 4 News whether this policy is racist, European Parliament member Dominik Tarczynski from Poland said, "This is why Poland is so safe. . . . We can be called populists, nationalists, racists . . . I don't care. I care about my family and my country." I'm not suggesting such a blanket policy based on religion is right for America, but it is a good example of the measures other countries take to protect their culture and people.

Neither am I suggesting that strong borders—even Trump's border wall—can guarantee America's safety alone, but secure borders, combined with clear, firm, and practical national security policies, can make catching and vetting those who try to gain admittance a hell of a lot easier. In other words, secure borders as well as stringent and enforceable immigration policies are necessary for America's continued prosperity. Everyone knows this, just as they know that the Biden administration is largely responsible for the ongoing national security and humanitarian crisis happening right now at our southern gates.

As of late October 2023, the time of this writing, around 10,000 immigrants per day are being apprehended along the border, most of whom are ultimately released into the United States. Who knows how many more are coming across undetected?

It's one thing to have a different opinion of how to handle a problem—most Americans get that. But when America's leaders deny that a problem even exists—all while citizens can clearly see it with their own eyes—it is another problem altogether.

IMMIGRATION POLICY

Now that we have the obvious out of the way, let's talk about policy.

Historically speaking, every prior administration—Republican and Democrat—has understood the dangers of lax immigration laws and porous borders. With just a few exceptions due to world wars and pandemics, both parties have always welcomed regulated immigration—as the historic record clearly indicates. After all, nobody denies that America is a nation of immigrants. Certainly, in recent years some administrations have differed slightly in their approaches to security, but no prior one has demonstrated such disdain for America's borders and established immigration code as the Biden administration has—and not just in words, but in actions.

Since we have limited space in these pages for remedial history, let's start in what some might consider the modern era, 1981, with President Ronald Wilson Reagan.

Ronald Reagan

The first portion of Reagan's tenure was defined by his "War on Drugs" initiative as the crack cocaine epidemic swept through inner cities. The federal government budgeted much more money for increased policing and more coordination between local and federal drug-interdiction units. The Anti-Drug Abuse act of 1986 called for increased penalties for those caught with illicit drugs; meanwhile, the federal government stepped up its role in preventing drugs from coming into America, mainly those coming from Colombia via Miami and the Gulf Coast.

Reagan made immigration reform a central theme of his second term; it was very important to him to allow honest and capable immigrants into the United States and to give those who were already here, and had proven themselves productive members of society, a path to legal citizenship, all while keeping ne'er-do-wells out and deporting any aliens who committed crimes.

In 1986, he signed the bipartisan Immigration and Reform Control Act (IRCA), which, among other things, provided amnesty and a path to citizenship for millions of unauthorized immigrants with clean records who could prove they'd been residing in the United States continuously since before January 1, 1982. He believed that providing a regulated and legal path for immigrants could decrease the number of illegal crossings.

The IRCA also mandated penalties for employers who knowingly hired unauthorized immigrants. The goal was to diminish the job magnet that attracted many immigrants to the United States illegally.

Third, the act increased border security by drastically upping the budget for the Immigration and Naturalization Service and the U.S. Border Patrol.

It's worth noting that at the time the IRCA was passed, Congress was controlled by Democrats, indicating that much work was done by Reagan to see that the bill was both compassionate toward immigrants who truly wished to assimilate into American society while at the same time being staunchly protective of America's interests. But of course, times were different in 1986, especially in terms of the polarization of politics and the power and influence of the Mexican cartels. Democrats and Republicans alike unanimously agreed that America needed secure borders, robust law enforcement, and policies that would make America safer for its citizens as well as those wishing to share in its promise.

George H. W. Bush

Just a year into his presidency, Bush signed the Immigration Act of 1990 into law. Notably, that law increased legal immigration quotas and introduced the Diversity Visa Lottery program, which allocated visas to individuals from countries with historically low rates of immigration to the United States.

Throughout his tenure, President Bush supported comprehensive immigration reform, like his predecessor, Ronald Reagan. However, efforts to pass such sweeping legislation during his presidency faced significant political challenges and did not result in major reforms. This, as you'll see, becomes a theme with all subsequent presidents.

The Sr. Bush played a crucial role in negotiating the North American Free Trade Agreement (NAFTA) among the United States, Mexico, and Canada. While not directly an immigration policy, NAFTA had implications for migration patterns and economic factors influencing immigration. If some didn't know it already, it proved that Mexico is a resource-rich nation and both a valuable partner and an ally—when its integrity isn't corrupted.

Bush extended the temporary protected status (TPS) label to individuals from countries facing ongoing armed conflicts or natural disasters. TPS provided temporary relief from deportation, as well as work authorization for eligible individuals from countries such as El Salvador, Honduras, and Nicaragua.

In sum, George H. Bush was a proponent of secure borders but also a big fan of immigration. Like every president before him, however, he tended to believe that America was a team made up of people who wanted to be on Team America. And as the head of that team, he wanted talented and loyal players of all positions. In essence, he wanted diversity. His innovative Lottery Visa and TPS programs, like other add-ons to Title 8, worked well, provided the current circumstances in America warranted them and that they contained strict requirements—standards—for accepting immigrants. Without standards, viable methods of enforcement, and consequences for cheating the system, any program can be exploited. There must be deterrence to ensure everyone plays by the rules, or else the team will suffer.

Bill Clinton

I'm always amazed these days when I talk to younger folks who seemed to be shocked that Democrats didn't always despise borders. While I didn't agree with President Clinton on many issues, he believed in strong borders, and I often cite him as my first example.

"We cannot tolerate illegal immigration, and we must stop it," said President Clinton. How's that?

Policy-wise, Clinton passed "Operation Hold the Line," a Congressional response to the increasing unauthorized border crossings from Mexico. Hold the Line—I don't know who comes up with these names!—involved deploying additional Border Patrol agents and resources along the United States–Mexico border in El Paso, with the goal of increasing border security and deterring illegal crossings. To decrease illegal immigration at the San Diego border he passed Operation Gatekeeper. Likewise he signed Operation Safeguard for Arizona.

He also signed an updated version of Ronald Reagan's IRCA in 1996; it strengthened immigration laws and had significant implications during his presidency, including provisions for increased border enforcement, employer sanctions for hiring undocumented immigrants, and penalties for immigrants caught trying to sneak in illegally, and it forged a pathway for legal immigration for certain undocumented immigrants who had been living in the United States since before January 1, 1982. Notably, it also included "Expedited Removal," a policy that gave jurisdiction to immigration officers to remove certain undocumented immigrants without a formal hearing or judicial review—primarily those apprehended near the border or within two weeks of unauthorized entry.

Throughout his presidency, Clinton's administration continually allocated resources and personnel to enhance border security. This included increasing the number of Border Patrol agents by 40 percent and improving technology and infrastructure along the United States–Mexico border.

In the 1990s, the Clinton administration faced a mini crisis with an influx of Haitian refugees and Cuban migrants. So, Clinton implemented policies such as the Haitian Refugee Immigration Fairness Act and the "Wet Foot, Dry Foot" policy under the Cuban Adjustment Act, which affected the treatment and legal status of individuals from these countries seeking asylum or entry into the United States.

Basically, Clinton was like all the other presidents before him; he knew the value of secure borders and a regulated immigration system for the nation's overall health, and his policies generally reflected that belief.

George W. Bush

U.S. president 43 often advocated for comprehensive immigration reform that would address border security, establish a temporary worker program, and provide a pathway to legal status for undocumented immigrants who were already in the country. In 2005, his newly formed Department of Homeland Security (created in response to the attacks of September 11, 2001) introduced the Consequence Delivery System (CDS) to increase the penalties for illegal border crossers if they were caught, in order to deter future attempts. In 2006, Bush's administration proposed the Comprehensive Immigration Reform Act, which included elements of these reforms. Like his father's attempts before him, the legislation faced significant opposition and did not pass in Congress.

What Bush did accomplish was increasing resources and funding for border security and enforcement efforts. Under his presidency, the number of Border Patrol agents increased, and technology, such as cameras and sensors, were deployed along the border to enhance surveillance capability.

In 2006, Bush launched Operation Jump Start, which involved the deployment of National Guard troops to the United States–Mexico border. The aim was to provide support to Border Patrol agents by assisting with surveillance, administrative tasks, and the construction of infrastructure. Nothing shows the cartels that you mean business by deploying guys in woodland camo fatigues, ballistic helmets, AR-15s, and American flag patches on their shoulders to secure the border and not just hand out water and direct people to Porta Potties; I sure hope the current administration remembers a little border history!

President Bush proposed the creation of the Guest Worker Program that allowed foreign workers to enter the United States legally for temporary employment. The program aimed to address labor market demands while providing a regulated system for temporary work.

If you thought Trump was the first to call for a physical border barrier, you'd be wrong. Clinton erected fencing in the mid-90s. Then in 2006, Bush signed the Secure Fence Act, which authorized the construction of fencing and vehicle barriers along the southern border. The act aimed to deter unauthorized crossings. Today, the barriers span about 700 miles.

Perhaps most significantly, Bush launched the Mérida Initiative in 2008. Mérida was a security cooperation agreement between the United States and Mexico with a stated goal of combating organized crime, drug trafficking, and related violence in Mexico and Central America. The heavily funded initiative looked to enhance the capacity of law enforcement and judicial institutions, promote the rule of law, and strengthen the capabilities of these countries via technology, intel, weapons, and enforcement.

Bush may have taken a lot of heat for WMDs, but he was a strong advocate of both secure borders and a robust immigration system.

Barack Obama

While you can't judge a politician by what he or she says, here are Obama's exact words on January 29, 2013, while talking about immigration reform at Del Sol High School in Las Vegas, Nevada:

> First, I believe we need to stay focused on enforcement. That means continuing to strengthen security at our borders. It means cracking down more forcefully on businesses that knowingly hire undocumented workers. To be fair, most businesses want to do the right thing, but a lot of them have a hard time figuring out who's here legally, who's not. So, we need to implement a national system that allows businesses to verify someone's employment status quickly and accurately. And if they still knowingly hire undocumented workers, then we need to ramp up the penalties.
>
> Second, we have to deal with the 11 million individuals who are here illegally. We all agree that these men and women should have to earn their way to citizenship. But for comprehensive immigration reform to work, it must be clear from the outset that there is a pathway to citizenship.
>
> We've got to lay out a path—a process that includes passing a background check, paying taxes, paying a penalty,

learning English, and then going to the back of the line,
behind all the folks who are trying to come here legally. That's
only fair, right?

So that means it won't be a quick process, but it will be
a fair process. And it will lift these individuals out of the
shadows and give them a chance to earn their way to a green
card and eventually to citizenship.

Compared to today's radical views on the left, Obama's sound reasonable to me. But what did Obama actually do?

In 2012, his administration introduced the Deferred Action for Childhood Arrivals (DACA) program, which provided temporary protection from deportation and work permits for undocumented immigrants who had been brought to the United States as children. DACA recipients, often referred to as "Dreamers," had to meet specific criteria to be eligible for the program.

In general, Obama increased border enforcement efforts along the same lines as Bush's, including the deployment of additional Border Patrol agents and technology to oversee border security. His administration focused on targeting individuals with criminal records or those who posed a threat to national security. Notably, he renewed Bush's Mérida Initiative but refocused it to place more emphasis—and funds—on criminal justice reform rather than law enforcement as the original Mérida Initiative mandated.

In 2014, he introduced the Priority Enforcement Program (PEP), which replaced the Secure Communities program. PEP aimed to prioritize the deportation of individuals who posed a significant threat to public safety or national security, rather than nonviolent immigrants.

Like other presidents, President Obama also advocated for comprehensive immigration reform. However, efforts to pass comprehensive immigration legislation, such as the DREAM Act, did not become law during his presidency.

So, in 2014, likely due to the lack of progress on immigration reform, President Obama announced a series of executive actions known as the Deferred Action for Parents of Americans and Lawful Permanent Residents (DAPA) and expanded DACA. These actions sought to provide temporary relief from deportation, and work permits for certain undocumented parents of U.S. citizens or lawful permanent residents. But these executive actions faced legal challenges, and their implementation was ultimately blocked by the courts.

Love Obama or loathe him, the man was no fool when it came to border policy. As far as his DACA policy, today most Americans agree with it. According to a 2020 Pew Research Center poll, 74 percent of all Americans support it. I agree with it as well; if a child was brought here illegally by an adult, it was not that child's choice. Kids are malleable, and most are eager to assimilate into American society, ultimately becoming part of the mosaic within its very fabric. After being ripped from their homeland once, only the hardest of hardliners would wish to rip them away again from the place they call home.

Where it gets complicated, however, are the cases where the parents (and many times, the cartels) know the DACA law and exploit it by using children as pawns. Therefore, we must thoroughly vet DACA kids to make sure they are legitimately displaced. But at some point, America must pass enforceable immigration laws, and most, including myself, are fine with DACA if the standard for application remains fair, honest, and equal and doesn't negatively affect those families who immigrate legally from the start.

It begs mentioning, however, that during his time in office, Obama was dubbed the "deporter-in-chief" by some who either were unhappy with his policies or liked to brag to conservatives that he was hawkish on border security. But the numbers don't (often) lie; roughly 12 million people were deported by Clinton, 10 million by G. W. Bush, and 5 million by Obama.[1]

Donald Trump

OK, so here's where it gets real for most of us, because we all just recently lived it by watching disingenuous report after disingenuous report on the news each day. Evidently some of us have short memories, because the fact is, Trump said nearly identical words as Barack Obama concerning immigration and border security, yet he was deemed a racist by the Left while Obama was deemed a champion of America and of humanity.

Here's what Trump did while in office:

Trump pursued trade policies to protect American industries and renegotiated trade deals such as the North American Free Trade Agreement (NAFTA), which was replaced by the United States–Mexico–Canada Agreement (USMCA). The number one underlying cause of illegal immigration is poverty, and so anything done to strengthen the economy of Mexico is a good thing for both Mexico and the United States.

He advocated for stricter immigration policies and border security; indeed, one of Trump's central campaign promises was to build a wall along the United States–Mexico border to enhance border security. "I will build a great wall!" he said repeatedly. While he faced challenges in obtaining funding for the wall from Congress, his administration did take steps to increase physical barriers. Existing border fencing was reinforced, and new sections of the wall were constructed.

In 2018, the Trump administration implemented a "zero tolerance" policy aimed at deterring illegal border crossings. The policy gave our immigration agencies the power to detain adults who had knowingly and illegally tried to gain entry, but it faced huge criticism by some who claimed that it separated families.

Early in his presidency, Trump signed several executive orders, including a travel ban placed on those coming from hostile, largely Muslim, Middle Eastern countries. It faced myriad legal challenges but was ultimately upheld by the U.S. Supreme Court in a modified form.

Trump implemented various measures to tighten asylum rules, including the implementation of the Migrant Protection Protocols (commonly known as the "Remain in Mexico" policy), which required individuals seeking asylum to wait in Mexico while their claims were processed. The administration also sought to restrict access to asylum for those who entered the United States illegally.

In a nutshell, President Trump campaigned on his "Make America First" platform, and it dictated his policy. He secured the borders, vetted immigrants while keeping them in Mexico, and was stern in his message that legal immigration was encouraged, while illegal immigration would result in stiff penalties. Although his zero-tolerance policy was ridiculed by the Left, who claimed that it frequently separated children from their families, much of the blame should go on the parents of those children who broke the law by trying to cross the border illegally.

Joe Biden

President Biden has eliminated dozens of immigration policies implemented during the Trump administration, including the "Zero Tolerance" and "Remain in Mexico" policies. In general, Biden has touted a "more humanitarian" approach to immigration, including increasing resources for processing asylum claims, expanded alternatives to detention for certain migrants, and sending the National Guard to hand out welfare items and assist with processing. However, many of these policies have proven anything but humanitarian for migrants.

Biden's administration modified a smartphone-based app—called the CBP One app—to modernize and expedite the immigration process. In actual practice, it makes illegal immigration easier and has been referred to by Republican members of Congress as a "concierge service" for illegal immigration.

Biden proposed a comprehensive immigration reform bill, called the U.S. Citizenship Act of 2021, that aims to provide a pathway to citizenship for undocumented immigrants, including Dreamers (DACA recipients), temporary protected status (TPS) beneficiaries, and agricultural workers. The bill is awaiting congressional approval and will certainly undergo heavy revisions during the legislative process.

President Biden often lectures political opponents on their priorities by stating, "Don't tell me what you value. Show me your budget, and I'll tell you what you value!" Well, guess what? While the Biden administration has said it is for better border security and management, it has allocated resources for enhancing border infrastructure, technology, and personnel dedicated to improving the processing of migrants and asylum seekers at the border while also insisting that money and resources not be spent on enforcement.

President Biden has emphasized the need to address the root causes of migration from Central America, including poverty, violence, and corruption. While he has proposed initiatives to provide economic aid to Mexico and at least $4 billion to Northern Triangle countries (Guatemala, El Salvador, and Honduras), his appointed "Border Czar," Vice President Kamala Harris, abdicated her position almost immediately following mainly ceremonial trips to both Central America and the border. While details of her abandonment are unknown to the public, what we do know is that she was not only ineffective, but disingenuous when she said, "The border is secure," on NBC's *Meet the Press* on September 11, 2022.[2]

In 2023, Biden's administration gave orders forbidding immigration agents to arrest illegal immigrants in America who are not convicted of violent crimes. This action further promoted the idea of the United States as a whole becoming a "sanctuary country."

Biden's reversal of the "Remain in Mexico" program while reinstituting "catch-and-release" before having a clear immigration and border security plan in its place has proven nothing less than catastrophic, or, as I wrote in an op-ed along with Katherine Kuhlman for *The Hill*: "One of the most incompetent homeland security decisions ever made."[3] I stand by this statement. Indeed, the 10 million-plus unvetted immigrants who have flooded into America so far during Biden's tenure have forever altered the country's demographic makeup.

Here's another fact: Biden's literal messaging (and messaging via his actions of reversing Trump's security policies) has convinced migrants that they are welcome to stay, legally or illegally, if they just make it over the border. Immigrants who are interviewed at the border often say this! One gentleman from Panama who wished to remain anonymous said via translation, "We don't know who the next U.S. president will be. But we can't believe there will ever be a better chance to enter the U.S. than right now."

The Biden administration's lack of an overall strategy has exacerbated more inhumane conditions than Trump's policies ever did. Most critically, these policies or lack thereof—along with a complete denial of the problem as a whole—have created the most dangerous threat to America's national security since the Cuban Missile Crisis. Of course, it's not hard-working immigrants who wish to make a better life here who are to blame—it's the crime, drugs, and terrorism that hide in the Trojan horse among them. Biden has left this monstrous problem squarely on the doorsteps of American taxpayers in cities and towns from coast to coast, and unless something changes, there's no sign of it stopping.

MEXICO'S IMMIGRATION POLICIES

At this point, it is worth taking a very brief look at Mexico's policies as well. After all, Mexico is the second most important player in this entire issue. As it turns out, today most of the immigrants are not from Mexico but are coming to America via Mexico from a host of impoverished Central American countries, such as the Northern Triangle, Colombia, Ecuador, and Venezuela. In total, immigrants from 170 countries are traversing through Mexico to reach the U.S. border. So, what policies Mexico institutes concerning its border security and immigration are of great consequence to us.

Although Mexico claims to have implemented measures to strengthen enforcement along its southern borders with Guatemala and Belize to curb irregular migration and human trafficking, we can see no positive results of it. Mexico claims that it aims to prevent unauthorized entry into its territory and regulate migration flows, but we know that it is letting people enter and traverse Mexico at will if they say they are planning to enter the United States.

Our southern neighbor has its own immigration enforcement agency, its National Institute of Migration (INM), which is responsible for controlling and regulating immigration within its borders. The INM claims to carry out inspections, detentions, and deportations of individuals who are found to be in violation of Mexico's laws. Mexico also *says* it cooperates with the United States in some cases of returning migrants who have transited through Mexico. In practice, however, it is falling short.

Mexico has established procedures for processing asylum claims and providing humanitarian protection to individuals who are fleeing persecution or violence. The Mexican Commission for Refugee Assistance (COMAR) is responsible for assessing and deciding on asylum requests. But due to resource limitations and increasing demand, the country of approximately 130 million people has huge problems in effectively addressing the needs of asylum seekers and refugees.

Mexico and the United States have, in the past, entered into various agreements to manage migration and border issues. For instance, the United States–Mexico border Partnership Action

Plan focuses on cooperation to enhance security, address transnational crime, and facilitate legal and secure migration. I mentioned Mérida, versions 1 and 2. The two nations also officially worked together on the "Remain in Mexico" policy, implemented by Trump in 2019. There have been others, some official and some clandestine.

Finally, Mexico officially says that it recognizes the importance of addressing the root causes of migration by promoting development in regions with high emigration rates and has tried to launch programs aimed at creating job opportunities, improving infrastructure, and enhancing security in areas prone to emigration, particularly in its southern regions.

What we know for sure is this: Mexico and the United States are inextricably linked. In 2022 alone, the two North American countries conducted more than $780 billion in annual cross-border trade;[4] tens of millions of U.S. and Mexican citizens are of binational families; more than 14 million people living along both sides of the nearly 2,000-mile shared border interact daily.

This increasing interdependency requires that both countries work closely together beyond the area of trade to institute an effective and coordinated strategy to diminish the shared threats that the Mexican drug cartels present to both countries' national and economic security, but it's difficult to do so, mainly because of the corruption that pervades the Mexican government. The cartels—who have a vast incentive to keep borders open or unsecure—have too much influence over its leaders. The bottom line is that both Mexico and the United States contribute to the problems of drugs, cartel violence, and illegal immigration, and it is in both countries' interests to solve them.

IMMIGRATION STATISTICS

Although presidents are politicians, and politicians often say one thing while doing another, the proof, as they say, is in the pudding (if we can trust the statistics given to us by official government sources).[5, 6]

Nationwide CBP Encounters by Encounter Type and Region: Fiscal Years 2014 to 2023 (September 2023)

Total CBP					
Fiscal Year	Total CBP	SW Land Border	Northern Land Border	Coastal Border	Air Ports of Entry
2014	711,666	570,048	31,016	56,637	53,965
2015	591,831	444,856	28,536	52,830	65,609
2016	690,433	558,991	26,788	39,990	64,664
2017	526,788	415,199	27,969	23,366	60,254
2018	686,070	519,944	34,131	22,269	109,726
2019	1,147,478	977,229	35,665	81,160	53,424
2020	646,799	458,082	32,373	113,287	43,057
2021	1,956,518	1,734,683	27,181	141,693	52,961
2022	2,766,580	2,378,944	109,535	163,755	114,346
2023	3,201,137	2,475,669	189,401	144,321	391,746

Notes: Southwest and Northern Borders include land ports of entry at those locations, and Coastal Border includes seaports of entry. Records may not match Component reporting due to differences in reporting methodologies. Data are current as of October 31, 2023; future reporting may include updates to previous reports' data.

Source: Office of Homeland Security Statistics Persist Dataset.

Enforcement Encounters					
Fiscal Year	Total Enforcement Encounters	SW Land Border	Northern Land Border	Coastal Border	Air Ports of Entry
2014	611,988	544,667	25,489	5,702	36,130
2015	471,289	403,473	24,173	4,403	39,240
2016	569,348	505,086	23,145	5,733	35,384
2017	456,668	385,192	25,014	4,582	41,880
2018	571,062	498,384	25,983	4,127	42,568
2019	1,021,803	957,409	18,358	4,631	41,405
2020	495,704	449,233	11,582	2,746	32,143
2021	1,783,744	1,726,947	12,619	2,463	41,715
2022	2,436,103	2,341,498	44,490	7,068	43,047
2023	2,641,704	2,457,266	135,892	8,821	39,725

Notes: Includes all USBP encounters, OFO encounters with dispositions other than those defined as administrative encounters, and encounters resulting in expulsion pursuant to the CDC's Title 42 public health order.

Source: Office of Homeland Security Statistics Persist Dataset.

Administrative Encounters					
Fiscal Year	Total Administrative Encounters	SW Land Border	Northern Land Border	Coastal Border	Air Ports of Entry
2014	99,678	25,381	5,527	50,935	17,835
2015	120,542	41,383	4,363	48,427	26,369
2016	121,085	53,905	3,643	34,257	29,280
2017	70,120	30,007	2,955	18,784	18,374
2018	115,008	21,560	8,148	18,142	67,158
2019	125,675	19,820	17,307	76,529	12,019
2020	151,095	8,849	20,791	110,541	10,914
2021	172,774	7,736	14,562	139,230	11,246
2022	330,477	37,446	65,045	156,687	71,299
2023	559,433	18,403	53,509	135,500	352,021

Notes: Includes specific types of encounters of inadmissible noncitizens in which removal proceedings are not considered, including certain withdrawn applications for admission in cases prior to FY 2024 in which expedited removal or other immigration proceedings were not considered, foreign crew members without entry visas who are required to remain aboard their ships, and persons paroled into the United States and released from OFO custody without being placed into removal proceedings.

Source: Office of Homeland Security Statistics Persist Dataset.

As you can see from the government-released statistics (assuming we can trust them), immigration and encounters were drastically reduced—even in the face of a humanitarian crisis in Central America—under the Trump administration. Trump stuck to his guns on his America First policy and worked with Mexico to develop programs that would keep immigrants in Mexico while they were vetted for parole.

Then the 2020 election happened, and Joe Biden immediately ceased construction of Trump's border wall and reversed the "Remain in Mexico" policy that had been so dearly needed. Every signal given to would-be immigrants was that the U.S. government would now accept all comers. And so, they came in droves. It was only until the news media and the administration could no longer act like all was peachy on the border that they finally released this statement by DHS Secretary Alejandro Mayorkas during an official White House Press Corps address on March 1, 2021: "We are not saying, 'Don't come.' We are saying, 'Don't come now. . . .'"

And with those words and a wink, the entire world received the message loud and clear: "Come on in; it'll be fine as soon as the political pressure dies down."

But why would the Biden administration differ from the attitudes and policies of every administration before it, regardless of party affiliation? That is one of the puzzles we will try to decipher, and solve, in the chapters to come. But first, let's talk about some of the crippling side effects that come with failing to properly label the crisis as it is: the gravest threat to American citizens and to America's national security.

CHAPTER TWO

Open
Border Threats

*Over and over again, I see other people talk about our
mission . . . and the context of it being immigration or the
current crisis today being an immigration crisis . . . I firmly
believe that it is a national security crisis. Immigration is
just a subcomponent of it, and right now, it's just a cover for
massive amounts of smuggling going across the southwest
border—to include TSDBs [those on the terrorist watch list]
at a level we have never seen before. That's a real threat."*

—Rodney Scott, former head of CBP while addressing
19,000 agents under his charge before being forced to retire
by DHS Secretary Alejandro Mayorkas on August 14, 2021

Geographically speaking, the United States is extremely
fortunate to be in the center of North America, bordered
on her north by a strong ally in Canada and that country's vast
wilderness, the formidable Pacific Ocean on her west, and the
mighty Atlantic on her east. Her only weak leak—mainly due to
corruption and a great disparity in economic wealth—is Mexico
to the south. Even so, the country is much better off than most

others that are landlocked with multiple tumultuous borders that must be always defended, not just in wartime. Certainly, America's geographical positioning has played a role in her continued prosperity.

Just remember back in World War II when Japanese forces attacked Pearl Harbor. The guarded Hawaiian Islands—some 2,500 miles from mainland America—were as close as Yamamoto's air and naval forces could get. Even when communism threatened our homeland in the 1960s by way of Russian missiles, the closest base of enemy operations was in Cuba, 90 miles away from our closest shore. Granted, that's too close for America's comfort, but it's highly desirable compared to, say, South Korea's position relative to its mortal enemy to the north, from which it is separated by airspace and guards with machine guns. It took Al Qaeda years of training, plotting, preparing, and failing again and again before it finally crashed a jet into the World Trade Center. In Jerusalem, similar acts happen rather frequently, partially because its enemies live within sight of their targets. Indeed, on October 7, 2023, scores of innocent women and children were slaughtered in southern Israel by Hamas terrorists who used paragliders launched from Gaza to initiate their heinous attack.

But times, technologies, and political winds have changed, with the result that America's geographical positioning no longer offers the dominant security advantage it once did. These days, America's enemies don't often begin assaults with outright frontal charges on its beaches or bombs over its ships' bows.

As I've said before, the old monster who you know is hiding in your closet is scary—but not as scary as the new monster who might be hiding under your bed.

While some threats, such as overt acts of terrorism, are easy to recognize after they happen, today's threats typically come in the form of subtle infiltration of American culture, sowing chaos in the form of social unrest and election interference, social media influence, profiteering from drugs and crime, addiction, and persistent subversion of resources—threats that can kill a nation like a thousand ticks slowly sapping the life from a country dog.

Although its cumulative effects are tough to quantify, Americans know they are being attacked because they can see it; those who can't physically see it can feel it. Certainly, for Texans, New Mexicans, Arizonians and Californians who have ranches or property near the border the signs of infiltration and danger at their doorsteps are glaring. They see illegals trespassing across their land; they catch them on trail cameras; they find litter; they discover their property has been damaged. Sometimes they find bodies. It's scary.

Yet, even for folks 1,700 miles away in Herndon, Virginia, who can't let their kids go to the public park due to the MS-13 gang-member meetings held at the pavilion, it's obvious, as it is for the thousands of citizens whose sons and daughters have overdosed at a party when they have unknowingly tried a drug that was laced with fentanyl. But for others—young men who need work mowing lawns, sheetrock construction guys, and housemaids—well-paying jobs are difficult to find, because many of them have been filled by illegal immigrants who will do them for much less than American citizens can afford to.

Can you believe that in July of 2023, Illinois lawmakers passed a law mandating that property owners may not refuse to rent or sell to illegal aliens? That sounds awfully compassionate

. . . until the illegal skips out on the rent, leaving the property owner with no recourse because, of course, the illegal alien has no documentation and cannot be found. As noted in several studies from both right- and left-wing groups, policies like this have certainly raised the already-sky-high cost of housing and will outprice many Americans in the years to come.[1]

According to a 2019 article by William La Jeunesse:

> . . 26 states offer [illegal immigrants] state-funded benefits. New York state offers up to $300 a month in cash assistance. Eleven states offer free or subsidized medical and hospital care. California offers food stamps, legal services, and benefits for those over 65 or disabled. Governor Gavin Newsom recently asked for an extra $50 million from lawmakers to serve the state's illegal immigrant population.[2]

A 2023 FAIR (Federation for American Immigration Reform) study estimates that illegal immigrants cost American taxpayers $150.7 billion per year, not counting the cost of border security. This is nothing short of economic warfare against U.S. citizens, brought to us by blue state officials and justified by pandering ideologies of inclusion!

Nevertheless, because so many Americans feel that there is nothing they can do about these assaults, they go on about their daily lives, hoping and praying that the government—those entrusted with the best interests of its citizens and national security—will make the right decisions and act. After all, elected senators take the following oath:

> I do solemnly swear (or affirm) that I will support and defend the Constitution of the United States against all

*enemies, foreign and domestic; that I will bear true faith
and allegiance to the same; that I take this obligation freely,
without any mental reservation or purpose of evasion; and
that I will well and faithfully discharge the duties of the office
on which I am about to enter. So help me God.*

But many of America's officials are breaking that oath. Indeed, even during its wars, America has never had to endure so many threats from so many different origins—even from within its own borders—all at once. It's all a bit overwhelming, really, especially now that many threats are masked by current social justice trends and even promoted under banners of diversity.

If America is to continue into the next millennia, however, all threats to her sovereignty and security must be systematically identified for what they are, and rejected by the American people, who then must implore their elected lawmakers to stop it via sound policies, practical enforcement, and dogged perseverance.

Let's examine some of the ongoing threats borne from open borders by revisiting a few news stories that have made national headlines over the past few years. After all, the American public should not have to lie awake at night wondering whom is being let into the country. Rather, we should know that our government is ensuring that those who want to do us great harm are not entering our communities with unfettered access. Unfortunately, under this administration, we do not have that assurance, for with each passing day more crimes are committed and more threats are uncovered:

- "Arrests of Suspected Terrorists at Border on Pace to Shatter Record," *The Daily Caller*, March 2023.

- "Feds Prevented Over 160 People on Terror Watchlist from Crossing U.S. Borders Illegally—Highest Total Ever Recorded: DHS," *New York Post*, September 15, 2023.
- "Biden Administration to Offer Work Permits to Roughly 470,000 Venezuelan Migrants," *Wall Street Journal*, September 20, 2023.
- "First Drugs, Then Oil, Now Mexican Cartels Turn to Human Trafficking," *NBC News*, April 29, 2020.
- "Texas Authorities Claim Mexican Cartels Murdering People on US Soil," *New York Post*, November 12, 2021.
- "Biden's DHS Sends over $770M in Taxpayer Money to NGOs, Sanctuary Cities Facilitating Illegal Immigration," *Breitbart*, August 23, 2023.
- "FBI Investigation Determined Chinese-Made Huawei Equipment Could Disrupt US Nuclear Arsenal Communications," *CNN*, July 25, 2022.
- "Open Border Fentanyl Deaths Equal a '747 Crashing Every Day,'" *Newsmax*, June 26, 2023.
- "Suspected Terrorists Crossing Border 'at a Level We Have Never Seen Before,' Outgoing Border Patrol Chief Says," *Washington Examiner*, August 16, 2021.
- "DEA Rocky Mountain Division Announces Record Fentanyl Seizures in 2022," DEA Press Release, January 9, 2023.
- "US Customs Officers Find Nearly 900,000 Fentanyl Pills Hidden in Shipment of Sinks, Authorities Say," *CNN*, July 2, 2023.
- "US Takes Action Against Chinese Companies, People Tied to Fentanyl," *Reuters*, October 23, 2023.

- "Sanctuary City NYC: Migrant Arrested 6 Times for Violent Crimes in 2 Months," *Breitbart*, September 4, 2023.
- "Authorities See Nearly 800% Surge in Chinese Migrants Crossing Southern Border Illegally," Daily *Caller*, August 18, 2023.
- "U.S. Deaths Due to Fentanyl Nearly Quadrupled in 5 Years," *U.S. News & World Report*, May 3, 2023.
- "How Mexico's Sinaloa Cartel has Flooded the US with Fentanyl," *Business Insider,* May 21, 2023.
- "Mexican Cartels Exploit US Government's CBP One App" *Washington Examiner*, August 4, 2023.
- "Watchdog Faults 'Ineffective' Border Patrol Process for Release of Migrant on Terror Watch List," *CBS News,* July 5, 2023.
- "American Citizens Being Turned Away So NYC Hospital Can Give Health Care to Illegals," *Western Journal*, October 12, 2023.
- "Chinese Using New Smuggling Route to Enter US Illegally: Report," *American Military News*, August 7, 2027.
- "MS-13 Gang Murder of Maryland Autistic Woman Sparks Investigation of Biden Administration," *Washington Examiner*, February 28, 2023.
- "Wielding Machetes and Baseball Bats, MS-13 Carried Out 'Medieval' Killings, Feds Say," *Los Angeles Times*, July 16, 2019.
- "Illegal Chinese Biolab Uncovered in California, What They Found Is Deeply Disturbing," *American Insider*, July 2023.

- "Biden Admin Threatens Banks That Refuse to Lend
  Money to Illegal Immigrants" *Daily Caller,* October 12,
  2023.

These headlines are a few of the hundreds like them that tick
across our feeds daily. To simplify, let's look at what our porous
borders and pathetic policies have gotten us.

By July of 2023, when this book was being written, we've
got fentanyl trafficking to the tune of about 70,000 American
deaths each year, not to mention the untold effects of all the
other drugs that cartels bring in, including other opioids,
cocaine, ecstasy, crack, meth, and everything else. (If you don't
think coke is literally everywhere these days, I'd remind you that
on July 2, 2023, it was found in Biden's White House! There's a
95 percent chance it came through Mexico to get there.) Then
there's the untold cost of crime, murder, addiction, healthcare,
and homelessness associated with all of it. There's human trafficking—modern-day slavery—that's become the cartels' dark
new billion-dollar business. In the case of forced prostitution
and child-sex slavery, this is truly one of the most abhorrent
crimes of them all. Yet, disgustingly, cartel business is booming.

What's more, by failing to secure our borders, we get the
particularly violent breed of Central American gangs who get
much of their money from drug deals as well as theft, carjack-
ings, kidnapping, robbery, and extortion through violence. Mara
Salvatrucha, or MS-13, is the most notorious, but there are others, such as Mara Máquina and Barrio 18, the latter of which was
also formed in Los Angeles but recruits heavily from the desperate classes of Mexico and Central America. Then there's perhaps
the greatest long-term threat to the United States, which is the
infiltration by democracy-hating terrorists who are intent on

destruction and mass murder, as well as Chinese and Russian nationals who specialize in espionage, sabotage, land grabbing, and stealing of trade secrets. And then there is the incalculable economic cost stemming from all of these criminal actions, as well as the hundreds of billions of dollars spent annually trying to combat them. And we haven't yet discovered some threats that are already being deployed by these nefarious groups and others who are on their way here. Just wait.

But for now, let's deal with the known monsters under our beds and the ghouls we've discovered in our closets.

A 2008 Department of Justice National Drug Threat Assessment report declared: "Mexican drug trafficking organizations represent the greatest organized crime threat to the United States." Since then, the problem has only gotten worse, and it continues to do so. By 2023, and due to the Biden administration's relaxing of border security policies, we are witnessing the heyday of the Mexican cartels.

THE HEYDAY OF THE MEXICAN CARTELS

As of the time of this writing, there are nine major cartels, and most are thriving. The Mexican government has proven it is ineffective and possibly uninterested in combating them, most likely due to internal corruption and/or violent intimidation. Pathetically, it seems the cartels' only real threat these days comes from rival cartels.

Here are nine of the most prominent, although we will go into more detail in Chapter 6.

- Sinaloa Cartel
- Jalisco New Generation Cartel (CJNG)
- Beltran Leyva Organization

- Gulf Cartel
- Los Zetas Cartel
- Juarez Cartel
- Tijuana Cartel
- Cartel de Santa Rosa de Lima
- Los Rojas Cartel

Unlike some notorious revolutionary groups of the past that used extortion through violence, kidnapping, and drug trafficking to fund their political ambitions, the Mexican cartels should not be classified as insurgents. To be clear, the cartels are criminal organizations with the primary goal of monetary profit through their criminal activities: illicit drug trafficking, kidnapping, human trafficking, money laundering, and extortion. The cartels do not want to rule the country or overthrow the government like, for example, the cocaine trafficking FARC group of Colombia did in the 1990s. Rather, their tactics are used to minimize governmental interference in their profit-making operations.[3]

MS-13 AND CENTRAL AMERICAN GANGS

"Transnational gangs, like MS-13, threaten our national security and the safety of our neighborhoods by ravaging our communities with violent crime and narcotics," stated HSI New York Special Agent-in-Charge Ivan J. Arvelo.

MS-13, also known as Mara Salvatrucha (*Mara* = "gang," *Salva* = El Salvador, *Trucha* = "street wise") is a violent criminal gang that originated in Los Angeles in the 1980s, founded by El Salvadoran immigrants. The gang has since expanded its presence and recruits primarily from El Salvador, Honduras, Guatemala, and Mexico. MS-13 is known for its involvement in various criminal activities, including drug trafficking and street-level dealing, human smuggling, prostitution, extortion, robbery, and murder. It often recruits young, impoverished, and impressionable boys, who are taught to use extremely brutal, imported methods of violence using machetes and knives.

The gang is thought to have 6,000 to 10,000 members living in the United States, with 60,000 or more abroad, and more coming into the United States each day. It is estimated to generate around $30 million dollars annually in revenue from drug and extortion rackets—ranking it well below many of the more organized Mexican cartels—although in 2012 the United States designated MS-13 as a transnational criminal organization (TCO), thereby putting it in the same class as the cartels.

Members are known to be heavily tattooed, even on their faces, although savvy new leaders are now tending to refrain from the facial tattoos, knowing that they make them much easier to identify. Others are more obvious.

The gang's loose structure made of neighborhood "cliques," each with their own independent activities, makes it difficult for law enforcement agencies to dismantle or eradicate MS-13 completely. Its transnational nature also poses challenges for international cooperation in combating its criminal operations. Governments and law enforcement agencies in affected countries have taken various measures to combat the gang, including increased police presence, intelligence gathering, and efforts to disrupt their financial networks.

MS-13 is terrifying not so much for its world-influencing power, of which it has little, but rather due to its juvenile, relatively small-scale, needless brutality that is often carried out on innocent civilians if a civilian unintentionally crosses them.

For example, in 2019, an MS-13 member of a northern Virginia clique, illegal immigrant Cruz Moreno, brutally shot a man in a wooded suburban area while Cruz's accomplices stabbed him, all because the victim was thought to have "disrespected the gang." This is not indicative of a billion-dollar Mexican cartel enterprise that does not want to draw undue heat onto itself by killing random American citizens, but rather a street gang doing what street gangs do when they are young, high, and looking to gain street cred. Despite many local cases like this one, MS-13 is to be feared on a larger scale.

In 2021, 14 of MS-13's highest ranking members, an inner circle known as the Ranfla Nacional, were charged with "terrorism offenses" in a New York court. While that came as good news, more members of this wicked, machete-wielding, tattooed crew are being granted entry into the United States under the Biden administration's CBP One app, which asks that these gangsters, by their own recognizance, simply show up for a court date to be determined years later. The trouble is, they are criminals, with no intent to ever appear in court. Finding them before they commit crimes—their daily business—is impossible. Yet, the current administration is letting them and other criminals into the country under the progressive banner of "humanitarianism."

According to former Chief of Border Patrol Rodney Scott, in an interview with the *New York Post,* when asked about the terrible position that CBP officers are being placed in by the administration's policies: "You know they are gang members, but there's no database to pass them off, and they won't admit it, so we can't document them as gang members. They're just getting released into the United States."[4]

We will get into those specific policies and law reversals in chapters to follow.

Being a father who simply wishes to raise my children in peace, the crime, murder, Schedule 1 drug proliferation, and human trafficking brought to American towns and cities by these brutal gangs probably scares me the most. And the Biden administration, combined with leftist, "no-bail" courts and defunded police departments, is making it easy for them not only to gain entrance into the United States but also to operate their heinous crime cliques and syndicates more efficiently from coast to coast and everywhere in between.

TERRORISTS

Title 22, Chapter 38 of the U.S. Code defines terrorism as: "Premeditated, politically motivated violence perpetrated against noncombatant targets by subnational groups or clandestine agents."

From January 2023 to September 15, 2023—the most recent data available at the time of this writing—United States–Mexico border agents caught 151 would-be immigrants whose names appeared on the FBI's Terrorist Screening Database (TSDB), commonly called the "terrorist watchlist." If this statistic does not sound the alarm to every American—especially considering the atrocious sneak attacks perpetrated by the international hate group Hamas on Israeli citizens in early October 2023—I do not know what will.

According to a September 2020 *Daily Caller* article, federal authorities "have flagged nearly 75,000 illegal migrants [already in the country] as potential national security risks."[5]

These numbers are simply staggering, especially when you consider that in 2019, under Donald Trump's watch, zero persons on the TSDB had been caught at the border. (During Trump's entire term, 11 persons caught crossing our borders were determined to be on the terrorist watch list.)

What's even more alarming is the following question that must be asked: If 151 people on the watchlist have been caught, and 75,000 more have been marked as suspicious, how many have not been caught? In other words, how many terrorists are living among us? How many are on their way here as you are reading this? Extrapolations from illegal immigration data suggest that many more have made it through to American soil than those who have gotten nabbed. The scary truth is our government doesn't have a clue.

What these terrorists are planning, however, is obvious. They do what they always do—like they did in October 2023 in Gaza and on 9/11 in New York City—and likely will *always* do: They will attempt to destroy American property, culture, and lives. *Who, where, how, and when* are the questions our law enforcement is now tasked with discovering. But with each passing day and 10,000 unvetted immigrants entering our country, our protectors' jobs get increasingly more difficult, if they are not already impossible.

So, what has happened between 2019 and now? It's obvious that with the change of administrations, terrorists have calculated that crossing the Mexican border presents them the highest odds of getting in. In the past, terror groups believed that recruiting sympathetic persons already living in America, or those who have or could receive legitimate work or study visas to enter the country, was their best bet. But now they calculate that it's easier to book a plane ticket somewhere in Central America, pay for a ride up, download the CBP One app, enter false information, and walk across the United States–Mexican border as if it were a bump in the road. And it seems their calculations are correct. Gee, thanks, Joe.

To be fair and transparent, however, I am not exactly sure where the people on the terrorist watch list are originating from, because the CBP is under a mandate not to reveal this information. Why? It's hard for me to conclude any other reason except that it doesn't wish to bias the American people against any particular group for fear of that group being discriminated against in some way. Once again, they are placing their progressive politics ahead of America's safety.

What we know for sure is this: Terrorists of all varieties can and do enter the country, as evidenced by 9/11 and by those who have been caught plotting terrorist acts.

In March 2022, an immigrant from Iraq, Shihab Ahmed Shihab Shihab was caught by undercover FBI agents and later indicted for plotting to assassinate former President George W. Bush as revenge for his role in the war in Iraq. Since 2020, Shihab had been living in Columbus, Ohio, but he planned to smuggle a team of ISIS assassins through the Mexican border to Dallas. The threat was legitimate, because Shihab had cased Bush's home and offices, among other evidence. What's puzzling is Shihab's immigration status. Although he was said to have immigrated legally under asylum claims in several reports, he was being investigated by the FBI initially for immigration/visa fraud when his evil intentions were discovered.

In 2014, Pakistani-born Tashfeen Malik, a devout Sunni Muslim, used a fiancée visa to immigrate to California, where she married U.S.-born Syed Rizwan Farook. Evidently, she moved to America with the sole intention of killing Americans. In December 2015, the pair opened fire on a humanitarian services center in San Bernardino, killing 14 innocent people before being killed in a shootout with police. She left a six-month-old baby behind.

These are just a couple recent examples of multiple terrorist plots and terrorist cells that have been uncovered. We should have known that they were possible within our borders from the very beginning. You had better believe that our adversaries are paying attention very closely to what goes on here in the United States, and if there's a chink in our armor and an opportunity to exploit our weakened national security, they will exploit it.

Some organizations, such as the Cato Institute, downplay the chances of an attack on U.S. soil by foreign born terrorists by citing historical statistics that suggest these types of attacks rarely, if ever, happen. I do not believe that historical statistics are reason enough to grow lax in the defense of our homeland, however. Indeed, just because the numbers of polio deaths are down, that is no reason to discontinue polio vaccinations. By the same line of thought, perhaps America's historically robust intelligence network, enforcement, and border security have kept the number of terrorist attacks on our soil low. Never should we grow complacent in our vetting and border security, but that is exactly what we are doing. We can expect the number of terrorists—and terrorist attacks—to increase in the years to come, just as we have witnessed from data collected at Biden's border. Remember when we declared, "Never again" after 911? Thanks for the advice, Cato, but I think we should lean toward being safe rather than sorry.

OPEN BORDER THREATS   45

If you're like me, it's mighty tough to rest easy knowing there are scores of extremist, anti-American individuals and groups lurking among us, biding their time for the perfect opportunity to commit a heinous act of terror. Others are *en route* now, licking their chops as they take advantage of our immigration laws for their own evil causes and nefarious desires.

Chinese Counterintelligence and Cartel Ties

Border Patrol has apprehended nearly 45,500 Chinese nationals crossing the southwest border illegally so far in an 11-month period of 2023.[6] The vast majority of these people are crossing our southern border not among family groups, but as unaccompanied adults. There is no doubt that the CCP is taking advantage of Secretary Mayorkas' open southern border, and every American should be alarmed.

We know that Chinese nationals are entering the border at a frightening pace—up 800 percent from just two years ago—and although we are not entirely sure why, we can make a few strong assumptions. Certainly, America has a checkered, nonglorious past with regard to Chinese immigrants, and it would do all law-abiding Chinese-born American citizens a disservice to not mention that. But the fact is that thanks to China's riches, its government's known willingness to ignore international law, its hunger for intelligence, and its strategy to "play the long game" of killing another country slowly by 1,000 cuts, this immigration threat cannot be ignored.

While I'd hope many Chinese immigrants are crossing the border illegally simply for the dream of a better life away from China's authoritarian state—just like millions of other people from 170 countries are doing—failure to scrutinize them could spell irreparable disaster for the United States. Let's face it: Honduras and Guatemala, for example, have neither the means nor the motive to pay huge sums of money to gather intelligence on the United States via spies posing as immigrants applying for asylum. China does. And China can use immigrants of other countries to get an advantage over the United States. This much has been proven.

In fact, there have been dozens of Chinese nationals convicted of spying for China and/or stealing trade secrets on behalf of their country within the last 10 years alone. Since 2017 specifically, the FBI has acknowledged a dramatic increase in espionage by the Chinese government on U.S. soil. Much of it has involved stealing trade secrets to gain an economic advantage over its number one world rival, while others are focused on learning the U.S. legal system and its media strategies so it can use them against us.

There have been many breaches in U.S. military capabilities via clandestine listening and video devices covertly installed by Chinese nationals at sensitive military and government installations. In fact, the FBI has documented over 100 cases of Chinese agents disguised as tourists near U.S. military sites. There have been suspect land purchases near U.S. government facilities, including near nuclear warhead launch sites in western states. The Chinese state owns large factories in America, of many industries, including agriculture. While these purchases might not be illegal on their face, they require persons with proper banking records to make them and boots-on-the-ground personnel for reconnaissance, all of which are the tasks of Chinese-sympathetic operators living here in the United States. Some of these are illegal immigrants. They must be stopped.

In 2017, under the guise of friendliness and "culture appreciation," the Chinese government offered the U.S. Arboretum in Washington, DC, $100 million to build an ornate oriental garden. The trouble was, after the U.S. counterintelligence officials reviewed the plan, it became obvious that the Chinese plan was to intercept transmissions from the U.S. Capitol. Many of these acts of espionage require U.S.-educated, possibly naturalized, Chinese immigrants to pull them off. Our first line of defense is our immigration policy.

While public trust of the FBI may not be at a high point now, it's tough to ignore the words of its director when he's privy to information that we are not.

"I will tell you that the Chinese counterintelligence threat is the greatest threat—certainly the greatest counterintelligence threat—that we face as a country," said FBI Director Christopher Wray during Congressional testimony.

In an interview granted to NBC News' Pete Williams, Wray said: "The scale of their hacking program, and the amount of personal and corporate data that their hackers have stolen, is greater than every other country combined." He went on to say that the FBI begins a new Chinese counterintelligence case every 12 hours. "There is no country that presents a broader, more severe threat to our innovation, our ideas, and our economic security than China does," he said.[7]

But there's more than just trade secrets and governmental espionage at risk: According to the U.S. Drug Enforcement Administration (DEA), fentanyl is a Schedule II controlled substance that is like morphine but 100 times more potent.

In 2021 fentanyl killed 41,587 Americans between 18 and 45 years old, making it the number one cause of death in that age group, even behind automobile accidents. Opioids such as fentanyl and oxycodone, account for 75 percent of all drug overdose deaths.[8]

According to the DEA, China is the number 1 source of the world's fentanyl, as it requires complex chemistry and is extremely difficult to make. It's little surprise then that most of the Mexican cartels' fentanyl either comes from China, is made after receiving ingredients and instructions from Chinese labs, or is produced by Chinese nationals living in Mexico.

Some authorities speculate that the Chinese-borne fentanyl scourge inside the United States is intentional. After all, China is a country that floods U.S. children's TikTok feeds with deadly trends such as the Blackout Challenge, Benadryl Challenge, Skull Breaker Challenge, Fire Challenge, Penny Challenge, Tide Pod Challenge, and others, but prevents the same content from being watched by its children in China.

"The Chinese Communist Party is involved in just about everything economically, businesswise, coming out of China, and you have Chinese scientists that have partnered up with the cartels," Sen. Marsha Blackburn, R-Tenn., told Fox News.[9] "China officially banned the production of fentanyl in 2019 under pressure from the Trump administration, pushing the Chinese drug manufacturers into Mexico, which is now a key part of the supply chain."[10]

No doubt, there are many factors at play in the fentanyl crisis, including the American-made market for it, education about its deadliness, and China's manufacturing of it. The CCP is taking advantage of Secretary Mayorkas' open southern border, and every American should be alarmed. If the United States is going to stem the flow of one of America's top killers—fentanyl—it must do it in large part by stopping it at the border.

ECONOMIC HARDSHIP AND STRAIN ON U.S. RESOURCES

What do all the aforementioned factors—exacerbated or caused by weak borders—have in common? In addition to killing Americans, they also weaken the U.S. economy. And while it's easy to discount the economic arguments, compared to losing actual lives, the fact that leftists do not often wish to confront is that weak economies are disastrous for humans in general. In general, poverty accounts for a giant portion of worldwide deaths, via a basic lack of food, shelter, clean water, and modern healthcare. Those who think a strong capitalist economy is bad might consider that the people of poor nations do not get to fight for equal rights, have abortions, travel, donate to charity, or buy luxury items such as organic food and electric cars, nor do they have the resources to care about issues such as transgenderism in sports or climate change. While money can't bring happiness to individuals, it can surely pay for top-notch healthcare and tickets to the Taylor Swift concert. Yet, our own flawed immigration system is bringing us down.

According to a study by the Federation for American Immigration Reform, American taxpayers pay nearly $162 billion yearly for services and benefits provided to illegal immigrants. According to the American Addiction Centers, the opioid epidemic alone has cost the U.S. economy $2.5 trillion in just four years. That's nearly 2.5 percent of the U.S. total GNP! And this doesn't account for all the other drugs that cartels traffic.

The cost of crime in the United States—from money spent on destruction of businesses, deaths, and costs of prosecution and incarceration—is likely about $4 trillion. While I can't pin all, or even most, of this crime on Mexican cartels and immigrant-based gang crime, some of it is. And it's only rising as our borders have disappeared and become a free-for-all.

As hard-working, proud Americans living in these hallowed states and raising our children the best we know how, it's an absolute abomination that we must worry about our kids becoming victims of gang violence, accidentally overdosing on fentanyl, getting killed by a random terrorist attack on a subway, or being kidnapped and sold into sex slavery, as happened not long ago to a 15-year-old girl who was attending an NBA game in Dallas. These days, we must worry about these things not merely in border towns or even while on vacation in Cancún, but in our great cities and quaint small towns in every corner of this nation.

We must make changes, and they must start with our government's reckless policies.

CHAPTER THREE

Politics and Policy

*Protecting the Nation's borders—land, air, and sea—from
the unauthorized entry of people, weapons, drugs, and
contraband is vital to our homeland security, as well as
economic prosperity.*

—U.S. Department of Homeland Security mission statement

E very administration since roughly the era after the Industrial
Revolution has held a similar outlook on immigration and
the securing of the border. While some naturally executed
their visions differently from others—depending on the economic climate and whether the world was at war—since Ronald
Reagan, all of them at one time during their tenures came up
with creative, detailed plans to address what they all knew was
an issue paramount to the nation's security and success: the
careful regulation of who enters and stays in the United States.
Some of these plans, written into bills, were passed into law,
while others were not. But they all had a common theme: to
enhance America by cherry-picking great people who are eager
to assimilate into American society, while at the same time protecting the country from foreign threats.

And then Bizarro World 2020 came along with COVID-19's lockdowns, and career politician Joe Biden eventually assumed the White House as its 46th president. Elected on a campaign slogan that should have been called "Anyone but Trump," since his first day in office, he has worked to reverse 88 immigration policies as of the time of this writing, July 2023. This sure seems like pretty weird behavior from a man who, while grilling then-President Bill Clinton's nominee for U.S. Attorney General Zoë Baird, said: "The committee and the public . . . has to be assured that you are, without exception, going to be willing to enforce the law. The immigration law falls under your responsibility; it happens on your watch as attorney general." (Baird's nomination was subsequently derailed by a scandal known as Nannygate, wherein Baird had hired two illegal aliens from Peru to look after her child.)

As you may recall from Chapter 1 in 2006, George W. Bush signed the Secure Fence Act, which installed 700 miles of border fence. You know who voted for it? You guessed it. Joe Biden.

However, one of the very first executive orders Biden issued after being sworn into office on January 20, 2021, was to shut down construction of Trump's border wall. "There will not be another foot of wall constructed [during] my administration," he said in an interview with NPR.

In 2008, as vice president, Biden is on video saying, ". . . people are driving across that border with tons . . . tons of everything from byproducts for methamphetamine to cocaine to heroin, and it's all coming up through corrupt Mexico."

So why between 2006 and 2020, would he change his stance on the building of a physical barrier? Some pundits on the right colloquially call it "Trump derangement syndrome," but quite seriously, Biden's flip-flop on this issue can only be explained by his and his supporters' rejection of anything Trump had enacted, simply for the political optics of it.

In poker there's a saying that when a player loses a big hand or two by being soundly outplayed, that person often begins playing irrationally—recklessly, with emotion rather than logic—in a desperate attempt to get his money back. Other experienced players can tell when a player is said to be "on tilt," and they use it to their advantage.

When Donald Trump shocked the Democratic establishment—and likely the world—by winning the presidency in 2016 in what was, by all official polls, supposed to be a landslide for Hillary Clinton, leftists went on tilt, and I believe they still are. Perhaps they simply wish to alter the current demographic makeup of the United States, or maybe they truly believe the United States can afford to help the entire world, but given the position switch, it's likely that they are making policy not by calculated, rational decisions based on data but rather by mantra of: "If it's Trump's policy, it must be bad, and therefore, we must reverse it."

There is very little evidence to suggest otherwise and plenty to back it up.

The effectiveness of Trump's policies, good or bad, could not have been thoroughly analyzed by the new administration, because it didn't have time to. Rather, they were voided purely out of spite. If they had been analyzed, Biden's team could have predicted the rush on the border it witnessed mere hours after the reversals were made.

You see, people of other countries tend to gauge the United States by its actions rather than the words of its politicians. Even if the Biden administration says it believes in secure borders, its actions—loosening the immigration laws and accepting almost all comers—broadcast a message that is translated clearly in any language: "Trump hates all immigrants, but we love them, so let them all enter."

It wasn't until March 1, 2021, after months of failing to acknowledge publicly what was happening at migrant holding stations on the border when DHS Secretary Mayorkas, speaking directly to the millions of immigrants *en route,* said: "We're not saying, 'Don't come.' We're saying, 'Don't come *now.*'" At that moment, he made it clear what the administration meant: It wanted everyone to enter America—just not when all eyes were upon the administration and the debacle they'd created on the border. It looked bad for them, because they'd criticized Trump for his immigrant holding centers that had been filling up more quickly than ever and spiraling out of control as illegal border crossers were briefly detained before they could be returned to Mexico. So, they wanted immigrants to wait until the launch of the administration's face-saving grace: the CBP One app—but more on this "Get in free" digital pass later. . . .

For this administration to pretend that its actions could have sent any message other than "All Immigrants Welcome" is absurd. Think about it: One day, there's a fence with a "Keep out" sign on the town's watermelon patch. The next day, after a new mayor takes office, the fence and "Keep out" sign are removed as the new mayor criticizes the former one for putting up the fence and sign in the first place. It is reasonable to expect a rush on the melons. And if the melons are all gone the next day, it can only be blamed on naivete, ignorance, or conspiracy. No one believes this administration is naive.

As further evidence, multiple anonymous human traffickers, when interviewed, told Reuters news service that the cartel traffickers were encouraging parents to send their children
across the border due to Biden's policy change of not rapidly
expelling unaccompanied minors.[1] Many illegal immigrants, as
evidenced on video by multiple reporters including the *Daily
Caller* reporter Jorge Ventura, personally thank our president
for the opportunity as they cross into America.[2]

Every administration prior to the Biden administration has
recognized that the United States has finite resources that can
be spent to combat illegal immigration, so historically most had
to choose where best to spend most of the effort. Most focused
first on border security to prevent illegals from entering, then on
removing those who are caught in the country illegally after committing a crime. When undocumented people commit crimes
and are caught (officially called *criminal aliens*), they show up on
police reports that land them on ICE's radar and are then investigated and often deported. But never has the United States let
immigrants into the country while the government tries to vet
them. The vetting has always been done before they enter, because,
of course, this makes the most practical sense. Until now.

As another example of the dramatic disparity even between
the immigration policy stances of Democrats in recent years,
consider that President Obama expanded George W. Bush's
Secure Communities Program that had cracked down on illegal
immigration.

The goal of Secure Communities was to enhance the federal government's ability to identify and deport undocumented
immigrants who had committed crimes. The program mandated that local law enforcement agencies would share the

fingerprints of people they arrested with the FBI and ICE. If ICE were to find that an arrested person were undocumented, it could initiate deportation proceedings.

The expanded program increased deportations, peaking at around 400,000 in 2012, and it prioritized the deportation of criminal aliens. Obama, for all the other issues I disagree with him on, did a very good job at deporting people who don't belong here.

Secure Communities did take some heat from the left side of the aisle, and it was, of course, lambasted for "racial profiling." (This is a typical tactic from the leftist playbook: ICE is directed to look for Mexican and Central American nationals coming across the border, but then it is accused of being racist because it tends to look for Hispanics. Critics call it racial profiling, but in my world, we call it "efficient investigation practices.") What the program was officially intended to do was to verify the immigration status of everyone who was arrested anywhere in the United States, regardless of race or skin color.

Caving from pressure, however, in 2014 Obama's DHS announced it would replace Secure Communities with the Priority Enforcement Program (PEP), which would focus on deporting serious (mostly violent, or major drug-trafficking) criminals. However, the Trump administration later reinstated Secure Communities in 2017.

But on January 20, 2021, Biden rescinded it.

Perhaps Senate Minority Leader Mitch McConnell summed it up best when he said, "It turns out when politicians spend a two-year campaign advertising a porous border and amnesty, people listen."

At least Biden and Co. made good on its campaign promise—especially good if you happen to be a drug smuggler, human trafficker, cartel boss, or terrorist ready to kill Americans.

DEFINING OPERATIONAL CONTROL

In my business—large-scale security—there's a term that we live and die by, sometimes literally: It's called "operational control." At a large sporting event like an NFL football game, for example, that means regulating the flow of attendees and/or having knowledge of everyone who enters and leaves the arena. In the case of U.S. border security, or very specifically, as defined by the Secure Fence Act of 2006, it means: "the prevention of all unlawful entries into the United States, including entries by terrorists, other unlawful aliens, instruments of terrorism, narcotics, and other contraband."

But, of course, having complete and total operational control in a country America's size, with so many personal freedoms, is impossible, so security professionals like me must adopt a more practical definition: We define border security as having *manageable* numbers of illegal immigrants. "Manageable" means having the manpower, tools, and resources available to confront, process, investigate, and deal with each individual immigrant accordingly.

All modern administrations prior to Biden's have maintained realistic and orderly control of our borders over most of their terms in office, because there has always been a consensus among the executive branch, the legislative branch, the judicial branch, and the American people that they must. This was nonnegotiable and funded appropriately by appropriations committees and then scaled up or down as needed to ensure it. But as of

2023, America has lost operational control of its own borders, and there is shockingly little effort being put forth to regain it.

While anyone can see this either by traveling to the border or by studying the statistics, then-acting Border Patrol Chief Raul Ortiz said as much during a House Homeland Security Committee hearing when he was questioned by Chairman of the Committee and U.S. Congressman from Tennessee Mark Green.

"Does DHS have operational control of our entire border?" asked Green.

"No, sir," Ortiz responded.

Despite what Mayorkas and the administration say (under oath, Mayorkas has said that DHS both does and does *not* have operational control of the border), the fact is, the U.S. government no longer has the appropriated resources or the proper plan in place to deal with each individual immigrant accordingly, as the law mandates.

Obama's Secretary of Homeland Security, Jeh Johnson, said as much in 2019 when he stated, "I know that 1,000 apprehensions overwhelms the system. I cannot begin to imagine what 4,000 a day looks like. So we are truly in a crisis."[3] If he thought that was a crisis, by late September and early October of 2023 the CBP reported around 10,000 border crossings per day, sometimes more. I suspect the number will continue to swell into 2024 as immigrants fear a less receptive president may be elected. (Lest you think Mayorkas was ignorant of all this, keep in mind that he was Obama's Deputy Secretary of the DHS.)

But what is most concerning is that the Biden administration has almost certainly *willingly* lost operational control of the southern border.

How can I say this without just sounding like a partisan hack? No doubt, there was unprecedented pressure placed on the border during Trump's time in office. Partisans and economists can debate the causes, but most believe it was largely induced by the economic collapse of several Central American countries while at the same time the American economy was booming. It's understandable that people fleeing one terrible situation, such as starvation in socialist Venezuela, would prefer to relocate to a place that has a surplus of food and prosperity. And so, Hondurans, Colombians, Salvadorans, Cubans, and millions of others have risked their very being to live decent lives here in America.

The difference between 2018 and now, 2023, is that Trump's words from the podium and his actions via policy (he campaigned on the promise of a border wall and increased deportations) sent a clear message that traversing America's border would be extremely challenging and tough, treading through desert, cactus, coyotes, rivers, and cartel turf. And he let would-be immigrants know that if they did manage to reach America, they wouldn't be welcomed with no questions asked, but rather they'd face strict Title 8 laws that identify and screen every soul to determine whether his or her claims of asylum is legitimate.

Trump worked a deal with Mexico so that the latter would accept large numbers of the migrant caravans (remember the caravans of 2019?) claiming asylum; even giving them medical treatment until their cases could be heard. Most were turned away permanently, as the stats show. Why were they turned away? It turns out, most of them did not want asylum in Mexico—which suggests many of these people weren't true asylum seekers trying to escape dire political persecution. (If you're trying to survive execution by a government firing squad, you duck and run to the nearest cover, which for many central Americans happens to be Mexico; you don't pack your bags and hire a guide to take you to New York.) Trump told them in direct, unambiguous language they should turn around. To match his words, he then ordered ICE and CBP to enforce the law; to do their jobs by turning illegals away at the border and by finding, processing, and deporting those who illegally made it in. Indeed, in 2019 alone, Trump deported nearly 300,000 illegals.[4]

Trump succinctly said in a speech given on November 1, 2018: "We've issued 40 million green cards since 1970, which means permanent residency and a path to citizenship for many, many people. But we will not allow our generosity to be abused by those who would break our laws, defy our rules, violate our borders, break into our country illegally. We won't allow it."

In stark contrast, the Biden administration campaigned on pledges to undo the "aggressive policies" of his predecessor and to implement a "fair and humane" immigration system. What he did was to completely dismantle it.

What happened to hopeful migrants because of Biden's ignorant policies—as time would tell—was anything but fair and humane, as seen in photos taken in immigrant detention centers and even more recently on the squalid streets of New York City, Chicago, and other sanctuary cities after being sent there. His policy reversals aren't in any way fair to American citizens either.

The new, progressive Left seems to forget that the Constitution allows America to make laws that protect its interests and national security even if it seems to be rude, offensive, unfair, or without full legal representation to noncitizens, just like other nations do to Americans. What the Constitution and the Oath of Office *don't* allow is issuing executive orders reversing established laws—edicts that have the net effect of decreasing America's national security. While the right and left political factions might disagree about the definition of "national security," it's difficult for most Americans to see how abandoning construction of the border wall, ending Title 42 with no plan of action in its place, restricting CBP's enforcement capabilities, and encouraging more illegal immigration by physically helping illegals cross the border could possibly be policies meant to enhance our national security.

In most Americans' view, according to polls—certainly my view garnered by years of training—Biden is guilty of losing operational control of the border and thereby decreasing U.S. security—likely out of spite for Trump and to keep his campaign donors happy. But I'll explore motives in depth later.

KEY POLICY REVERSALS, ALTERING THE LAW, AND THE CBP ONE APP

On his very first day in office, after using executive action to cease construction on the wall, Biden rescinded Trump's ban on immigrants coming from seven troubled Middle Eastern countries (and two others) including Iran, Libya, Iraq, Somalia, Sudan, Syria, and Yemen. (Iraq was later removed from the list.)

The Left spun this policy as a racist "Muslim ban," since most Muslims tend to be of Middle Eastern descent, and it was immediately challenged in court by the American Civil Liberties Union and the National Immigration Center on behalf of other pro-immigration groups.

But this simplistic view discounts the fact that individuals of other religions who were nationals of the listed countries were also subject to the same travel restrictions as Muslims. Likewise, individuals of the Muslim faith who were nationals of countries not listed in the travel ban were unaffected.

Want specific proof? People from Venezuela and North Korea were included in the ban; you just didn't hear that from the media. If anything, the policy singled out the fact that foreign-born terrorists overwhelmingly originate from these countries. Yes, it's unfortunate for most Middle Easterners, who just want a better life of freedom in America, but we can't ignore the fact that a significant number of Muslim extremists want our complete and total annihilation in accordance with their perceived religious beliefs. We can argue all day long about that last statement, and we can even bring up the name Timothy McVeigh, but the fact is, currently it tends to be Muslim extremists who are responsible for the most terrorism worldwide.

The U.S. Supreme Court agreed, and in 2018 upheld Executive Order 13780/Proclamation 9645, in its third rendition, ruling that it fell within the president's authority to regulate immigration for national security reasons. Biden dashed Trump's efforts with the sweep of a pen.

Of all the policies that Biden nixed, however, the Migrant Protection Protocol Act, aka "Remain in Mexico," has proven to be the most consequential.

The Migrant Protection Protocols (MPP) was a U.S. government action officially announced in December 2018, during the Trump administration. It significantly altered the way the United States handled asylum seekers, particularly at the United States–Mexico border.

Under MPP, individuals arriving at the U.S. border or entering illegally who were seeking asylum were returned to Mexico to wait for the duration of their U.S. immigration proceedings. This included individuals who were not Mexican nationals but who had traversed Mexico to arrive at America's southern border. The goal was to deter false asylum claims and ensure that individuals with legitimate claims could be processed more quickly.

When Biden killed it, it instantly let asylum seekers who crossed the United States–Mexico border proceed into the United States—regardless of the validity of their claims. It also encouraged millions more to come, literally—as we discovered in mid-2023 via the daily news—by the literal trainload.

As I previously mentioned, many of these folks claiming asylum from Central American countries didn't want to live in Mexico. So, now that they knew they could bypass Mexico and come directly to the promised land, why wouldn't they?

The administration also expanded the definition of "asylum" and altered the protocols for legal immigration claims without congressional approval.

For a little history, U.S. immigration law is written so that the United States accepts immigrants who can contribute to American society and do not immediately need charity. Historically, that's been the American way, and immigrants, including our hardy immigrant relatives, understood this. They might not get a free ride or government handouts, but once in and legally naturalized, they can take advantage of America's unique freedom to work hard, get an education, climb the ladder, and achieve the American Dream. Bootstrapping it is not easy, but regardless of what many socialists say, it's real. All of us know people who have risen from rags to riches under America's system.

Section 212(a)(4) of the Immigration and Nationality Act (INA) addresses the grounds of inadmissibility for immigrants to the United States. This section is commonly known as the "public charge" provision. It reads as follows: "(4) Public charge (A) In general—Any alien who, in the opinion of the consular officer at the time of application for a visa, or in the opinion of the attorney general at the time of application for admission or adjustment of status, is likely at any time to become a public charge is inadmissible."

The provision is meant to prevent individuals from immigrating to the United States if they are deemed likely to become dependent on public assistance and government benefits. If a consular officer or the attorney general believes that an applicant will be unable to support themselves financially or will rely heavily on government aid, they may be denied a visa or entry into the United States.

Historically, attorneys general took this provision to mean that any immigrant who immediately needs welfare should not be admitted. There is no quicker way to empty the welfare coffers than by giving funds to those who have never paid taxes but immediately need welfare. And once they're emptied, who will suffer? The same folks who always suffer the most from bad domestic policy: the poorest American citizens.

But, oh my, how things have changed! Indeed, Mayorkas and Co. seem to think needing welfare is the main reason immigrants should be allowed entry, and that giving them welfare once they're in should be the highest priority. Right now, millions of immigrants, both illegal and those following DHS CBP One app instructions, are in U.S.-provided hotel rooms, brought there by U.S.-provided buses and jets, given taxpayer-funded food and healthcare, all while using U.S.-provided cell phones. It's madness.

So how can they get away with it? Perhaps it's best explained by Simon Hankinson, the Heritage Foundation's senior research fellow in the Border Security and Immigration Center, in an op-ed for Fox News:

> [In] 2022, the Department of Homeland Security redefined "likely at any time to become a public charge" as "likely at any time to become primarily dependent on the government for subsistence, as demonstrated by either the receipt of public cash assistance for income maintenance or long-term institutionalization at government expense."
>
> This means that immigrants can still take a raft of federal, state and local benefits yet not be judged ineligible for a visa. I've processed thousands of immigrant visas and almost none were refused under the public charge ineligibility.[6]

And to add insult to injury, you can guess who now pays the tab—right down to the immigrant/asylum application fees—even if the claims are rejected. Yup. You and me.

How else has this administration dismantled the protections Trump put in place? Well, for one, it began secretly auctioning off parts and components of Trump's border wall for peanuts, even as the wall's ultimate construction fate remains in the courts. (As an addendum to this statement, in October of 2023, under heavy political pressure the Biden administration began rebuilding parts of the wall, no doubt having to buy more materials they'd sold for pennies on the dollar just months prior.) On May 11, 2023, the administration ended Title 42, which, when active, gave the U.S. Customs and Border Protection a legal way of repelling immigrants at the border by invoking this 1944 law that was intended to prevent the spread of communicable diseases in times of national health crisis. From April 2020, when President Trump's Title 42 took effect, until May of 2022, when it was rescinded, it stopped approximately 1.8 million would-be asylum seekers and potential COVID-19 carriers from entering the country.[6] When Title 42 was rescinded, there was an even greater mass rush at the border, because immigrants knew they would be processed in the United States, and not returned to Mexico, as the U.S. immigration code reverted to Title 8 law. This came as a surprise to no one.

On top of reversing Trump's Remain in Mexico policy and Title 42, in May of 2023 the Biden administration modified and implemented its technological, political problem-fixing *pièce de résistance*: the CBP One mobile app.

The CBP One app is a smartphone-based immigrant initial-processing app that, in effect, allows illegal immigrants to enter the United States by merely downloading it, entering some information, clicking the "asylum" button, and setting up an appointment with an officer who is supposed to then give them a date for a parole hearing sometime in the future. Then they can confidently waltz into a border-crossing station to enter America "legally." To be clear, it's "legal" only according to the new executive action surrounding the app, but it's technically *illegal* under existing U.S. immigration code. Therefore, I'll continue to classify CBP One users who have entered the country, but have not been paroled, as *illegal immigrants*. While inside the United States they are free to do whatever they want until months or years later, when they are expected to show up for their hearing. Those early arrivers who received early hearings and who were granted parole appear to have been paroled in mass batches, rather than individually, as the U.S. Code mandates, judging by the number and speed at which they were adjudicated. It took me hours to get a new license plate at a DMV despite having all my paperwork ready. Do we really think that 1,600 asylum seekers can be individually vetted in a day as the administration claims it is doing in 2023?

I'd argue that America isn't a KOA campground. This "digital immigration honor system" that is the CBP One app is digital-age insanity. It's like Willy Wonka's golden ticket. More accurately, the app is a dream come true for pro-immigration advocates, criminal aliens, and cartels alike, for many reasons:

- It encourages more immigration.
- It gives illegal immigrants some type of legal standing—a virtual visa—if they are caught.
- It makes immigration easier.
- It lends the administration justification (in their minds, anyway) for classifying these people as legal, rather than illegal, immigrants.
- It grants the administration a convenient tool to clear the migrant holding centers for which they so heavily criticized Trump. (Who needs holding centers for vetting if there is no vetting?)

The trouble is that the clearing of the detention centers is just a shell game wherein the illegal immigrants are moved around among our cities by our federal government so that they are harder to see, tougher to count, and therefore more difficult to blame on the Biden administration.

With the app in hand, illegal border crossers can skip the lines, the laborious legal immigration process, and the detention centers. And why wouldn't they if they could live wherever they wanted in America, just by downloading an app on a cell phone and entering whatever information they wish, as if it were an immigrant's version of Tinder?

Few would argue the viability of a thoroughly designed and tested immigration app if its goal were to reduce paperwork and introduce new forms of digital biometric vetting that were previously impossible. If it were meant to be downloaded while in the immigrants' countries of origin and used to digitally submit their immigration requests, documentation, verified biometric information, and asylum claims—all to be doubly verified in-person later—I could see how something like it could be very useful. I'm an advocate of using technology to our advantage. But it's now being used as a presidentially issued (albeit technically illegal) license to skip the line to enter America.

According to language pulled from DHS' website, "Since its launch on January 18, 2023, through the end of June, more than 170,000 individuals have successfully scheduled an appointment to safely and orderly present at a designated POE [point of entry.]"

What these numbers indicate is that even still, only a relatively small number of border crossers are using the app when we consider that several million people have entered America since that time. According to U.S. House of Representatives Judiciary Committee data it published in a report:

> Between January 20, 2021, and March 31, 2023, the Biden
> Administration has removed from the United States only
> 5,993 illegal aliens who were encountered at the southwest
> border and who were placed in removal proceedings before

an immigration judge during that time. In other words, of
the at least 2.1 million aliens released into the United States
since January 20, 2021, the Biden Administration has failed
to remove, through immigration court removal proceedings,
roughly 99.7 percent of those illegal aliens.[7]

Perhaps illegal immigrants believe it's even easier to hop the border in-between POEs than to download the app. If so, it likely means that our border security is even more pathetic than we might think. (Or maybe it's because the app is as glitchy as its users report, or maybe both.) But more on the CBP One app later.

Next, to make it easier for these border rushers to stay in America, the administration reinterpreted the legal language of Title 8 to accept asylum claims based on fears of gang violence and even domestic violence. Such fears, of course, allow asylum to nearly anyone, because anyone can claim they've been a victim without having to show proof. And sadly, domestic violence is rampant in the world. If a person is a victim of this despicable treatment, we'd all hope they would leave the situation or seek help from those who are in an immediate position to help. But experiencing domestic violence cannot be, and never has been, a license to move to America . . . until now.

Furthermore, the administration reinstated the Deferred Action for Childhood Arrivals (DACA) program, which protects people from deportation if they arrived in the country as children.

This is a tough issue, because kids who get ensnared by their parents' bad decisions too often are made to suffer. Antagonists of this policy argue that it has been proven to encourage parents and traffickers to send kids across the border alone, which, of course, leads to human trafficking. Mountains of anecdotal evidence from traffickers and victims alike support this argument. We will have to tackle this complex issue after the border is secure.

The craziest part is the administration reversed the rule that mandated background checks on DACA arrivals and sponsors! There is no explanation for this reckless policy; it's irresponsible at best, unfathomably dangerous at worst. Plenty of cartel-hired kids and MS-13 members are under the age of 18. To let this age group in without a background check is insanity. And to fail to conduct background checks on the guardians in America who will receive these poor, vulnerable kids invites exploitation of the worst kind imaginable. Familial DNA testing was used to verify whether the people who claimed they were the family of the child were, in fact, the family. I simply cannot understand the administration's reasoning for discontinuing the background check and DNA-testing program—when possible—on anyone entering America or receiving immigrant children. If they think it's a human rights violation, I'd remind them that American citizens submit various types of biological information over the course of our lives. Real human rights violations are when cartels smuggle children to sell their bodies to anyone offering money.

In 2021 and again in 2022, Biden greatly expanded the number of immigrants eligible for temporary protected status (TPS), allowing time-limited permission to enter for people of El Salvador, Nicaragua, Yemen, Afghanistan, Somalia, Syria, and Sudan, and, more recently, Cameroon, to name a few. As of April 2023, there are approximately 673,000 people on the TPS list either in the United States or awaiting entry.[8]

But perhaps the single most egregious edict the Biden administration has given has been to neuter America's Border

Patrol, largely turning it into an immigrant-processing and -aid organization that helps immigrants with their paperwork and sees to it that everyone is safe with plenty of access to food and drinks, healthcare, shelter, and power to charge their cell phones.

In effect, Border Patrol agents' hands are zip-tied. Their duties have been shifted from protection and enforcement to humanitarian aid. That is why, rather than preventing illegal aliens from crossing the Rio Grande, myriad images and news videos show our Border Patrol helping these aliens across, in much the same way as the National Guardsmen were instructed to do when 1,500 of them were sent to the border in the days before Title 42 was set to expire. (These troops were strategically sent under the guise as "security" and for a dog-and-pony show photo op to calm the American people, when in fact they were, by law, not allowed to act in an enforcement or protection capacity but rather to hand out snacks and direct traffic.)

Today, Border Patrol agents find themselves in the same hopeless situation daily. In fact, agents who signed up to protect the country from foreign invasion are leaving the force in droves. The suicide rate among the Border Patrol ranks is spiking.

As one nameless agent said, when asked what he does when confronted with an illegal immigrant who demands to enter the country: "We can't say no."

While we have barely scratched the surface in terms of past immigration policies the Biden administration has destroyed in just three years, we must ask ourselves the trillion-dollar question: Why?

POLITICS OVER NATIONAL SECURITY: WHY DEMOCRATS HATE TRUMP'S EFFECTIVE POLICIES

We've already covered why I believe this administration uncritically removed all of the former president's immigration policies: out of pure spite. But there are a few more factors that I believe play a major role in these dangerous policy decisions.

The first is the fact that Biden and the Democrats in charge are beholden to activist groups and special interests, including immigration advocacy groups and nongovernmental organizations. NGOs often pose as religious organizations or humanitarian charities, but most are pro-immigration political activist groups whose main goal is to see America fundamentally changed—often to socialism. These are the concierges—the administration's de facto travel service—who are hired to receive the immigrants from cartels (or by any other means) and place them in cities and towns all over the country. (In late 2023, DHS admitted to an Arizona congressional delegation that it was releasing approximately 5,000 immigrants per day to NGOs who then help them land in destinations inside the United States.)[9] These covert maneuvers (remember the midnight flights?) are often done with taxpayer money in the form of government grants. Turns out, Biden made many promises to many of these groups on the campaign trail, and now they're calling. It's big business for them, as they are a vital cog in the gears of human trafficking, and the administration is paying them billions to do it via funds from agencies such as the Department of Homeland Security, Health and Human Services, and many others. This also provides the administration a way to veil the taxpayer money spent on transporting, housing, feeding, and processing immigrants, because if it is spent as a grant, it is easier to hide in annual budget reports. Now it appears the administration is funneling money to NGOs from funds earmarked for FEMA. Seems to me like that money could be going to Hawaii right now, after the devastating wildfires ravaged it.

It's a racket, and I believe it's one of the reasons the administration hates prior tough-on-immigration policies and seems to relish those that let more immigrants into the country at will. It's a way to scratch the backs of the NGOs that scratch theirs.

As I was writing these words in late August of 2023, I saw this headline from Breitbart: "Biden's DHS Sends over $770M in Taxpayer Money to NGOs, Sanctuary Cities Facilitating Illegal Immigration." Author John Binder is exactly right. This injection of taxpayer money is not going to solve any problems in these sanctuary cities; rather, they are merely going to encourage more illegal immigration. In essence, Americans are being forced to fund their own demise.

IDENTIFYING NGOs

Here are a few NGOs, some of which are paid by the federal government—i.e., you and me—to facilitate mass immigration. It is very difficult to find specific information about them, their finances, and their activities. This is by design.

- International Organization for Migration
- International Rescue Committee
- Vera Institute of Justice
- The Refugee and Immigrant Center for Education and Legal Services (RAICES)
- Lutheran Immigration and Refugee Services
- The American Civil Liberties Union (ACLU)

- Bipartisan Policy Center
- Young Center for Immigrant Children's Rights
- Asylum Seeker Advocacy Project (ASAP)
- ActBlue
- Border Angels
- Kids in Need of Defense

It has been an ongoing theme of the administration to change the roles of border security institutions to appear to be combating illegal immigration while in actual practice encouraging more of it.

Perhaps Border Patrol Agent and National Border Patrol Council President Brandon Judd was correct when he said during an interview: "We could stop this tomorrow. We don't need more money. We don't need to throw more money at NGOs. We do not need the taxpayer to shoulder this burden. All we must do is put proper policies in place. . . . If we went back to policies like Remain in Mexico, this would end tomorrow. But they don't want it to end."

Judd continued: "Look at all of the political appointees that are in the West Wing. They come from activist backgrounds. Look at DHS, the political appointees in DHS. They come from activist backgrounds. They do not come from serious backgrounds that want to do right by the American people."[10]

Other than using NGOs to mask the true use of taxpayer money, fulfill its pro-immigration agenda, pay off its election debts, and keep the billion-dollar racket going, there's likely another reason this administration wishes to fill the country with needy immigrants—and it's one as old as democracy itself: Democrats hope to turn each immigrant into a Democratic voter, thereby strengthening their hold on the control of the country. Many of us believe that's a major reason why they intro-duce legislation to hasten the path for immigrants to become citizens. Hell, in some parts of the country—Illinois being one of the most recent—there are bills on legislatures' floors that would allow noncitizens to vote! Biden has vowed to back the powers of state and local governments to defy federal law when it comes to sanctuary cities, thereby providing a place for ille-gals to stay without fear of reprisal.

What's undeniable is that this administration will stop at nothing to stay in power, including using the DOJ to silence and even jail its political opponents, as well as decreasing the national security of the entire nation by letting unvetted ille-gal immigrants enter—all in the name of power. Meanwhile, anyone who opposes their pro-immigration, America second policy is called a racist, a xenophobe, and a bigot for not being more empathetic to immigrants.

The radical Left has implemented policies and erased oth-ers that fly directly in the face of the Department of Homeland Security's mission statement listed at the beginning of this chap-ter. It has single-handedly dismantled America's historically robust border security and its policies, all in a gamble for polit-ical control of the country. It has given the perception to those who are willing to make the dangerous trip to the border that our country's immigration laws will not be enforced. And why do officials fail to enforce specific laws? It's when they don't like them. In other words, they *want* mass immigration.

If I haven't provided enough clues as to why they want it, I'll take a deeper dive in an upcoming chapter. What we do know for sure is that the administration's continual failure to even acknowledge the scope of the crisis at the border—instead

proclaiming white supremacy and climate change as more serious threats—is a slap in the face to all Americans.

Not long after Biden took office, the administration insin-
uated that unless we have immigration reform, the border can't
be secured. But as a security expert, I know the exact opposite is
true: We can't have immigration reform until the border is secure.

How do we do that? Read on.

CHAPTER FOUR

Every Town a Border Town

Every city in the country is now becoming a border town.

—Katie Pavlich, editor, Townhall and Fox News contributor

A socioeconomic phenomenon occurs when two communities of wildly disproportionate wealth are divided by a firm political border. That is, people of the poorer, less-prosperous community tend to migrate into communities of greater economic prosperity if they can. It's a component of humans' natural quest for survival—Maslow's Hierarchy of Needs–type stuff. Where there is more food, water, shelter, safety, and opportunity for living and luxury, humans tend to go. This we know.

The problem is that the space where two economic classes collide often creates an economic vacuum wherein one class discovers a market for certain products and services. Within this more prosperous market, they can often make much more money for the same goods sold than they would if sold in their own market. At the same time, the wealthier class often feels an opportunity to take advantage of the labor, goods, and services that are priced lower due to the country's currency value, its average income, and myriad other economic factors. Basically, it's a win-win for both seller and buyer until equilibrium is reached.

For example, if a car in the United States costs $25,000, that same car might cost $20,000 in Mexico. So, if someone in Mexico can purchase a car for $20,000 and smuggle it across the border, he could sell it for $24,000, making $4,000. Meanwhile, the buyer is happy, because he saved $1,000. Certain medical procedures are another example. Simultaneously, many common goods such as groceries, sporting equipment, and electronics may often be cheaper in the United States prompting enterprising people to buy them in the United States to sell in Mexico. Such transactions happen thousands of times each day when legal and illicit goods and services are peddled across our southern border.

For a more relevant example, consider that as of 2023, a gram of cocaine in Colombia sells for $4, whereas a gram in the United States sells for around $70. Certainly, there are other factors in play that make this drug more expensive in the United States than just Americans who can afford to pay more for it, but the effect remains the same: If you're a drug cartel or a street dealer selling coke, where would you rather sell your product? I'm neither a coke dealer nor an economist, but I know the answer to this riddle. And it's the same for everything from human trafficking to day labor.

The other result of clashing economies is often crime. After all, cocaine is illegal in America, so of course the act of selling it is a crime. More broadly, where one side is desperate for money and goods, and another side has a surplus of them, you can bet that both legitimate and criminal enterprises will be active, trying their best to move the rarest commodities to the ripest markets in exchange for money, even if this means illegally crossing political borders. In plain, criminal terms, it often equals more violence that is inherent with selling illicit goods.

Anyone who has ever been to the border towns of Brownsville/Matamoros, El Paso/Ciudad Juárez, Heroica Nogales/Nogales, or San Diego/Tijuana, to name a few of the most notorious, knows this socioeconomic phenomenon to be true. As further evidence, I'll point to the U.S. border with Canada. These two countries are very similar in terms of economic prosperity, and so there is much less incentive for illegal trading across the border. When crossing into Canada from the United States or vice versa, the only warning you can expect to receive is "Watch for moose." I fully realize that not all U.S./Canadian border towns are safe. But what I can tell you is this: As a father, I'd much rather see my college-age kids celebrate spring break in Vancouver than in Matamoros.

Yet, until recently, crime that we've come to know as "border town–style crime," such as human trafficking, kidnapping, and street-level extortion has been generally isolated to border towns and mainly those on the Mexican side. I believe this was mainly because while criminal elements (once called *banditos*) could slip across the border to sell their contraband and then return home, they didn't *live* in the United States, because the United States' stiff anti-crime/drug/immigration laws and enforcement made it very difficult for alien criminals to do so. So, the crimes committed by banditos in the United States tended to be on or near the border. But this is rapidly changing as cartels and foreign criminal elements spread their networks from coast to coast, border to border. And these networks are growing in size and scope as they find it easier and easier to infiltrate.

There's a stark difference from years past when Border Patrol agents, Texas Rangers, U.S. Marshals, and ICE agents were mandated to aggressively seek out, pursue, and incarcerate border-hopping criminals, compared to today, when Border Patrol agents are ordered to discontinue chasing illegal border crossers if they reach high speeds. Others are relegated to computer processing, directing foot traffic and handing out water as illegals flood their posts.

Today, leftist, pro-immigration policies have combined with defunded police departments to create the perfect storm for crime and lawlessness in America.

CRIME IN AMERICA AND THE IMMIGRANT EXACERBATION

The Left picked a hell of a time to defund the police.

In 2020, as the immigrant crisis at the border was snowballing, and Biden was handed the reins to the Oval Office, urban liberal enclaves around the country began reducing the budgets of their police forces after "human rights" activists began destroying entire city blocks by rioting in the streets, looting, encouraging violence, and desecrating property in the name of "fairness and equity." Portland is the most infamous example, but there are many more.

How anyone thinks that shrinking the presence of law enforcement in areas that are most ravaged by crime could possibly improve those areas is beyond the mental capacity of most critical thinkers. Of course, no one does. *Better* policing, yes. But *less* policing? No way.

The brain-dead "Defund the Police" movement was concocted by activist groups such as Black Lives Matter and local politicians to win the favor of their inner-city protestor constituents by making it seem as if they were taking action after the high-profile police killings of George Floyd, Eric Garner, Michael Brown, and others.

Sadly, however, the people in these high-risk areas are the very people who need *more* policing in their communities—and *more* money for *quality* policing—the most. Statistics show that where law enforcement presence is minimized, violent crime generally rises, and vice versa. Of course, proactive policing means that the areas with the highest crime will likely experience more arrests of its criminal citizens, and unfortunately, some innocent ones along with them, so it's likely the police won't win many popularity polls. But having an unpopular police force is often better than an ineffective one, where good people are afraid to leave their homes for fear of the violence that awaits them outside their doors.

I'll frame the "Defund the Police" movement this way: If someone were truly racist and therefore wished ill will on the people of minority and/or impoverished communities, they *would* call to defund the police there, because it's an action that would directly hurt those communities most. No one in my political circles is calling for that, because it is evil.

It seems the only people who are calling for less policing are the mayors, politicians, and other officials who represent the most impoverished districts, live above the fray, and don't need constant patrolling in their gated communities. They have ample security; what they need are votes. Again, it's all about political optics for these people, not about actually solving problems. In this case, though, their actions are causing more problems for the people they pretend to be helping.

To be sure, with the open border policies and the mass influx of unvetted illegal aliens being bussed and flown to cities around the United States, the crime situation in America is only going to get worse. If racial tensions are bad enough now, try dumping tens of thousands of homeless Latino and Muslim minorities into cities that already have significant racial problems and whose own citizens can't find decent jobs. Newsflash: It's happening right now as I write these words.

America simply cannot accept this burden upon its resources without feeling it in its economy and infrastructure. And who will feel it most? The same people who most need quality policing—those Americans who depend on taxpayer-funded welfare and charity systems to get by. The middle class will also feel it. Those who are too well-off for welfare, but too poor to exploit tax loopholes, always bear the brunt of taxation.

Even New York City Mayor Eric Adams, once a proponent of accepting more immigrants into his city, is waving the white flag, saying, *No mas*. As of early August 2023, the city's homeless shelters are overwhelmed with more than 100,000 illegal aliens from the southern border, many of whom are sleeping cheek-to-jowl in the streets of Manhattan after the government-funded (i.e., taxpayer-funded) hotels have filled up. Several giant recreational centers, and even wings of public schools, have been transformed into shelters for immigrant overspill. What about the kids who used to play ball there instead of playing on the dangerous city streets? No matter.

Mayor Adams said this crisis will cost New York City taxpayers $12 billion over three years. Here's another sobering newsflash: The city can't afford $12 billion. So, who will pay? That's right. The federal government. You and me.

"We have run out of room," said Adams.

Sorry, Mayor Adams, but it didn't take a genius to see this debacle coming. You are a vocal advocate of sanctuary cities, and therefore you had a hand in making the bed in which you now sleep. But, oh, how quickly these ideologically motivated leaders flip-flop when their beds become soiled.

Now that crime rates are skyrocketing—even by New York City's standards—and he has no more room nor money to house more immigrants, Adams doesn't know what to do except to beg the federal government to do *something*. I find it appalling that he's asking the feds to do something for the illegal immigrants; what about his citizens and *legal* immigrants who have had their lives upended by this invasion?

If you think the term "invasion" is a cruel exaggeration, just look at some of the photos coming out of that city right now, or, better yet, go there yourself. It's strange how many of the *poor, orphaned DACA kids with no families and nowhere to live* have prison-house-style, murderous teardrop tattoos about their eyes while flashing gang signs for the cameras.

I can say with 100 percent certainty that this influx of non-tax-paying "asylum seekers" is burdening the good citizens of New York City by lowering their quality of life, altering their daily lives, and even taking from their children. It's not good for the immigrants either, who should have been directed by the administration to get in line, pay their dues, and immigrate the legal way. In fact, many of them now are refusing to go to the shelters that have been set aside for them, claiming that the shelters are even worse than the living conditions they left. Some of them are even going back home. This alone should both alarm Americans while simultaneously proving that many of these aren't fleeing persecution but rather seizing an easy opportunity.

Even Adams was finally forced to admit what we've all been screaming: "Everyone's block is going to be impacted by this," he said in a rare moment of clarity brought about by desperation. "We have to add our advocacy with our ability to help our neighbors, and we need everyone on board with this. . . . Our schools are going to be impacted. Our healthcare system is going to be impacted. Our infrastructure is going to be impacted."

In essence, the Big Apple, one of America's cultural crown jewels, is quickly becoming a border town.

But trust me, New York's elite (the people who call the shots in that city) aren't big fans of border towns; I've heard many urban elites bad-mouth the great immigrant buffer state of Texas at every chance they get. But finally, now that immigration is affecting *them* in a negative way, we are beginning to hear the complaints of NYC's finest liberal celebrities. It turns out they like the *idea* of open borders, free immigration, peace, love, and happiness for all—just not when poor people show up near their ritzy stoops and block their paths to the nearest Starbucks.

Similarly, on August 8, 2023, Massachusetts Governor Maura Healey declared a state of emergency as 20,000 immigrants bulged her state's shelters, costing taxpayers $45 million per month while adding crime and raising the cost of living. Keep in mind, Healey is also a proponent of sanctuary cities. Or at least she was.

"The declaration serves as a notice to the federal government and the Commonwealth that the state's shelter system is rapidly expanding capacity in an unsustainable manner, and that further assistance is urgently needed," said Healey's official press release.

It gets much crazier. Both Adams and Healey had the audacity to ask their residents to *house* and provide for illegal immigrants. That's right, they called upon residents to provide free room and board. Even though residents would be breaking federal law by giving quarter to aliens who entered the country illegally, the bigger question is this: Are Adams and Healey, who live in big houses with private security, housing any immigrants in their homes? Surely, they are! What about the city council? Fat chance.

Add Chicago, San Francisco, and others to the list of leftist-run sanctuary cities that are calling for assistance from the feds as well. (Chicago officials are threatening to start busing migrants to the suburbs! I wonder how that will go over!)

Despite the drop in tourism that these cities are likely to experience, it's not these places—which have large-scale infrastructure available—that worry most Americans. Blue state cities, to an extent, are rather used to chaos, drug problems, rampant crime, and homelessness. This is the price they pay for their liberal laws and lax policing. Quite frankly, many of the affluent people who live there seem OK with the trade-off, or else they would move.

It's the smaller cities, and even towns, that will be completely upended by surges of migrants that they, from an infrastructural standpoint, are simply incapable of accepting.

These immigrants may be poor, but they are not stupid. In fact, I believe impoverished people, who have historically had to make do with whatever they have access to, largely due to corrupt governments, are some of the most resourceful people in the world. They will go to areas with less stress on resources, and by doing so, they can inadvertently stress the resources there that are unprepared for the influx of people. While most of these people are not criminals by trade and will carve out niches for themselves and their families and live in peace, some are. Crime rates will rise. Bet on it. Is this fair for American families? You decide.

Although many border towns have lower violent crime rates than many of America's most notorious cities, when compared to interior towns only a few miles away, America's southern border towns tend to have more crime. It's just the way it is. Until Mexico gets its economy running to its full capability and reins in the cartel influence, that's the way it will be into the foreseeable future. Yet, that shouldn't mean that average American towns and mid-sized cities that historically have been wonderful places to live must experience the same border town–style problems. But I'm afraid that is what is happening. And we can't blame it all on immigrants.

Certainly, the human and fentanyl trafficking issues are relatively new problems instigated by cartels and their illicit trade across the border; but the influx of immigrants is also exacerbating existing problems that left-wing policies, politics, and ideologies created. As for the Right, it is also not without blame. It should put its money where its mouth is by refusing to pass any legislation in the Republican-controlled House—including aid to various other countries—until there is meaningful change to what is America's most pressing problem. It also must address the mental health issues—a common refrain of the Left—that are at the core of America's incessant drug problem.

SIX BIG REASONS WHY CRIME IS INCREASING ACROSS AMERICA

Policies related to the overall abandonment of law and order are a major catalyst of everything this country is currently experiencing that is related to the overall deterioration of civilized society. These days, it's not uncommon to see people robbing, assaulting, and looting in broad daylight, without fear of punishment. Simply put, what we are witnessing are horrible federal policies feeding into more atrocious policies at the local level. The border crisis, combined with the "Defund the Police" movement, have created the perfect storm for America.

Disenfranchisement of Law Enforcement Personnel

If rank-and-file police officers are unduly persecuted for doing their jobs or trying to, they are less likely to do their jobs well. Many have been fired for refusing COVID-19 vaccination or have been laid off due to defunded budgets or for being noncompliant with new woke policies mandated by city officials.

California was the first state to mandate officer training in sexual orientation, gender identity, and appropriate terminology. Other states are following suit. What these things have to do with decreasing crime is anyone's guess.

Other officers have quit out of personal danger to their lives, due to feeling handcuffed by policies that give every advantage to the suspect, both on the street and in the courtroom. Others have quit out of disgust after risking their lives to catch a criminal, only to see him or her be released back onto the streets soon afterward. As most of us have witnessed on the news by now, some "woke" cities in effect let gangs of thieves brazenly steal from retail stores by passing no-pursuit laws and/or downgrading the theft of goods valued at under a certain monetary threshold (in California's case, $950) to a misdemeanor.

Not only does this embolden criminals thereby causing more crime, but it also destroys the businesses that hire people from those communities and provide the residents with goods and services. It also pummels police and citizen morale. Just read a small portion of a resignation letter written by 26-year Portland police veteran Stephanie Hudson:

> . . . *Portland has a mayor who refuses to call out ANTIFA and condemn the riots, a DA who refuses to prosecute violent rioters and a Council Member who accuses police of committing the arsons and violence that were committed by the rioters. All of these previously mentioned people blame 'right-wing extremism' and the police for the violence and destruction in Portland.*

Similar letters are being written by law enforcement professionals in Democrat-run cities throughout the country.

The net effect of the disenfranchisement of police is that cities are less safe and totally unequipped to handle the influx of drugs, human trafficking, gang violence, and the crime that accompany open borders. In sum, Americans are less safe.

Of course, what these cities need is more policing and bigger budgets to promote more training. I'm talking about actual police training such as force-on-force training, better training in less-lethal tactics, intelligence gathering, de-escalation techniques—not for more feel-good "woke terminology" classes that help no one. They need more money to hire more high-caliber police officers and to train them professionally. Then they need district attorneys to prosecute swiftly, yet fairly, those who break the law.

A Weakened Economy

The U.S. economy is on a downward slide, thanks in large part to the "anti-inflation" bill that, as any nonpartisan economist knows, effectively exacerbated inflation. Even Joe Biden admitted that the "anti-inflation" bill was inappropriately named.

"I wish I hadn't called it that, because it has less to do with reducing inflation than it does to do with dealing with providing for alternatives that generate economic growth," said Biden in an address to wealthy donors in Park City, Utah, on August 10, 2023. Yeah, we know, Joe.

When the government prints money and defaults on its credit, inflation must follow. Every honest economics textbook explains this. Inflation means that things such as bread, medicine, and gas cost more. And when people get desperate for basic goods needed for living, when their paychecks suddenly don't cover their basic needs, crime tends to increase. When jobs are tougher to come by, crime increases. And when the disparity between the rich and the poor increases, crime increases.

Look for this vicious cycle to continue as taxpayers are forced to pay the tab for millions of illegals when that money could be going toward new schools. Taxpayers are already feeling it. The amount of money being paid by American taxpayers to fund illegal immigration—non-Americans—not even considering the momentous toll levied upon American resources, infrastructure, jobs, businesses, and policing—is staggering.

Racial Tension

When an administration says that "white supremacy" is the biggest threat to national security, there's a decent chance many people will believe it. When one group blames another group for taking what it sees as its jobs—whether this blame is aimed at Asians, Latinos, Jewish immigrants, or whomever—racial tension rises. And when racial tension rises in places where different races live near each other, people-on-people crime tends to increase. I'm not telling you anything you don't already know. Ninety-nine percent of us hate true racism and are doing our best to stamp it out. Certainly, it exists in America as it does the world at large. But to say that white supremacy is the *biggest* to the American homeland as Biden said during a commencement speech at Howard University in 2023—when we have statistics and experts that say otherwise—is not only a race-baiting lie, but a dangerous one.

Influx of Illegal Immigration

In addition to people, open borders allow more drugs, human trafficking, terrorism, and gang activity into America. We've covered this, so I won't beat the horse again right now, but facts are facts. Large-scale fentanyl trafficking, human trafficking, and transnational criminal organization (TCO) activities are, combined, at an all-time high right now in America, and it's no coincidence that crime is spiking.

Creation of Sanctuary Cities

The term "sanctuary city" describes a municipality that has adopted policies limiting cooperation with federal immigration enforcement agencies. Sanctuary cities are an invitation for illegal immigrants, including those involved in crime, to move across the country with impunity to seek refuge from the federal immigration code. Once there, many illegal immigrants are ill-equipped to find honest work within America's system, which requires a social security number or tax ID, and so they are taken advantage of by those who are looking for cheap and often untaxed labor. Others must resort to crime to get by.

Certainly, many find under-the-table cash jobs, but doing so, by code, is a crime.

Today more than ever, criminal elements find it easy not only to cross the border, but also to move freely throughout the United States and live here permanently. Traditionally, these illegals lived in larger cities, where the markets are larger and it's easier to blend in, but this is changing rapidly as more immigrants enter the country. Some places are being invaded by criminal foreign nationals.

Take Herndon, Virginia, for example. Twenty years ago, this suburb 25 miles from Washington, DC, was a quaint little town in Fairfax County. In 2018, Fairfax County Sheriff Stacey Kincaid cut cooperation with ICE by terminating its Intergovernmental Service Agreement and stated that Fairfax would no longer "honor any requests to detain individuals subject to an administrative detention request unless there is a corresponding lawfully issued criminal detainer."

Now Herndon and other towns in the county, like Manassas, are flooded with alien criminals. Indeed, Herndon is the home of several high-profile MS-13 gang murders that have taken place in the last several years. Some Americans in those neighborhoods have ceded their city and moved out. Thanks to these sanctuary city laws, today alien gangsters don't even have to hide. Why would they, when they can move in, invited with a guarantee of no criminal deportation for entering?

But when it comes to sanctuary cities, the national capital is, of course, California, where Governor Gavin Newsom rules from his fortified office and mansion, protected by 24-hour security, unbothered by crime and chaos that his policies have unleashed. Again, it's the middle and lower classes—the people who have to live there because they do not have the means to escape—whom these policies affect most.

The economic toll these leftist free-for-all policies are creating is almost incalculable. Productive citizens and business owners are leaving the state in droves, citing that the crime rate and taxes are simply overbearing to their freedom and quality of life. Since 2020, literally hundreds of businesses have moved their headquarters elsewhere, as have wealthy individuals—job creators—such as Joe Rogan, Elon Musk, and countless others. Meanwhile, Newsom is using taxpayer money to pay the attorney fees of illegal aliens who desire legal representation. If that's not an America Last policy, I don't know what is!

Appointment of Radical Progressive Judges and Revolving-Door Courts

Judges who release violent felons back onto the streets with minimal punishment should be removed—if lowering crime is the goal. According to the Bureau of Justice Statistics, the recidivism rate for convicted criminals is 77 percent within five years of release. Think about that: *Most incarcerated criminals commit crimes again after they are released.* In a nutshell, if judges wanted lower crime rates, they would scrutinize criminals before releasing them back into the general population. Plenty aren't doing that.

Cuban-born Los Angeles County District Attorney George Gascón, whose campaign was bankrolled by Hungarian-born George Soros, is one of the most notorious for letting career criminals walk in and out and in and out of the revolving door of his court. These are almost exclusively radical left-wing judges who have been installed by activist organizations after they realized that it's easier to place people into power who can choose not to enforce the laws than it is to actually *change* the laws. And we're not talking minor drug offenses here, as I think most people can reasonably understand why a person convicted of selling a bag of weed 20 years ago probably shouldn't be still sitting in prison when marijuana is largely legal now. No, I'm talking about violent felons who are dangerous predators living and lurking among honest people.

As B. D. Hobbs of KTRH News Radio of Houston said in 2021:

> *With the crime rate at a record level high here in Houston, most of the egregious violent crimes all have one thing in common. They were committed by a criminal who was out on bail after multiple incidents. A repeat offender of the worst kind. So why does this keep happening? Why do career felons with lengthy rap-sheets continue to be set free to commit more crimes? The short answer is liberal judges, working in partnership with liberal DAs.*

In fact, many of the jurisdictions that are plagued the most by violent crimes committed by repeat offenders are the same ones whose political leaders are pushing to do away with cash-based bail systems so that offenders can get out of jail for free as they await trial. Chicago, with one of the highest violent crime rates in the nation over the last decade or more, is one such jurisdiction.

Leaders of these jurisdictions insist America's bail system is racist. But this should be a slap in the face to the vast majority of African Americans and other minorities who do not commit crimes. Cash bail is not racist, it's anti-crime. Most crimes are committed by repeat offenders. Cash bail keeps the honest residents safer by preventing repeat offenders from committing more crimes while they await trial.

Certainly, America's court systems are far from perfect, and they can be unfair to those without money to pay for the best lawyers. Some are rife with abuse, good ol' boy networks and unequal justice, and therefore many need to be overhauled. But most citizens believe that letting violent criminals loose to walk around committing more crimes is the definition of insanity.

By a simple internet search, I could cite hundreds of examples where violent criminals were released by judges and went on to commit murders, rapes, and armed robberies, but let's get back to our border problem. . . .

THE PERFECT STORM

While all of the aforementioned factors (and more, such as white-collar varieties) contribute to crime, most of the *violent* crime—in the most dangerous places in America—tends to be among the inner-city streets of impoverished neighborhoods. (Why this statistical fact is rarely addressed by leaders of those neighborhoods is another story altogether.) Nevertheless, drug and dangerous gang crimes, which were once thought of as inner-city problems, are rapidly coming to the suburbs and even small towns as criminal gangs and cartel influence spread out in search of untapped, fertile markets.

In sum, when we combine bad border policies with defunded policing, we should not be surprised by more crime and the exacerbation of existing crime . . . and ultimately, all-out lawlessness. America's Great Promise is one based on personal freedom, to be sure, but we can only be free to exercise our God-given rights where there is a modicum of order and decency.

The effects of illegal migrants, drugs, weapons and continued human trafficking will certainly spread as numbers increase. And we have yet to fully understand the added negative consequences of surreptitiously relocating migrants across the country, placing them in cities whose officials and citizens are unaware of their presence.

And then there is the economic impact. According to a study by the Federation for American Immigration Reform, American taxpayers pay $150.7 billion yearly for services and benefits provided to illegal immigrants.[1] Make no mistake, a perfect storm is brewing, as these issues are inextricably linked.

With violent crime escalating across major U.S. cities while police departments are being straitjacketed by local politicians, morale among many of our law enforcement agencies is crumbling. It is no surprise that agents and officers are retiring and resigning at record rates or relocating to other departments where they can use their training to prevent and respond to crime. Now, local communities also must manage the influx of migrants spread across them and the issues that result. Future administrations must recognize that ensuring the safety of its citizens is their primary job.

Until America becomes so undesirable that even criminals don't want to live here, the only things standing in the way of more of these vicious, gun- and machete-wielding, tattooed gangbangers making their way to your community, or one near you, are robust border security and strict policies that enable law enforcement to find them, incarcerate them, and/or deport them whenever and whenever they are caught. If they make it across the border, it's up to your local law enforcement and district attorneys to see that they are incarcerated if they commit serious crimes.

Only your voice and power through polls can reverse the recent spate of anti-American policies before it's too late. For if the flow of criminals bent on robbing America, and terrorists determined to destroy it, is not mitigated, you can bet that, over time, more towns—even those geographically nowhere near the border—will become border towns.

CHAPTER FIVE

"Gotaways" and the Unknown Threat

You don't have a brain if you don't think we need to secure our border.

—Oklahoma Governor Kevin Stitt, August 21, 2023

Illegal immigrants who come across our borders are classified by CBP into one of three buckets

1. Encounters
2. Known gotaways
3. Those never detected

While there are glaring, serious concerns with all of these groups, and all of them are potentially threats to our national security, the last two are the most alarming.

The "encounters" consist of illegal migrants whom CBP apprehend while they unlawfully try to sneak into the country in between the ports of entry, as well as those who claim asylum via ports of entry. As any honest Homeland Security expert will tell you, the problem is that there is no feasible way to vet millions of encountered migrants thoroughly. Our system is simply not designed for that type of volume. Further, many countries do not share background information with the United States and/or do not maintain reliable systems and databases. This means that if an illegal migrant has not previously come in contact with U.S. authorities, and information is not shared by their country of origin, there will be no way to vet them thoroughly. This is often the case and would typically lead to denial of entry into the country. However, under this administration, it's "Come on in!"

Even Bill Clinton said as much in mid-2023: "The [U.S. immigration] system is built to handle about 400,000 [annually]." The years 2021, 2022, and 2023 each averaged around 2.8 million, or roughly seven times the amount Clinton says our system can accommodate. Very likely it's even more.

In addition to the manpower, processing centers, and data systems needed to handle millions of would-be immigrants, another problem stems from the fact that we do not share information with certain adversarial countries like China or Iran (and many others), or those that lack the security professionalism, technology, or infrastructure to track background data of its citizens *to* share. As I always say, any vetting we conduct is only as good as the systems that we are vetting *against*. In other words, if many of these migrants have not previously come in contact with U.S. authorities, they likely will not appear in our systems. Still, very few who are encountered on the border and let into the country are currently being deported.

The answer, of course, is to not let anyone into the country once our processing capability is maxed. I'm sorry if this causes consternation for would-be immigrants, but if we are to value security for the American people over the desires of noncitizens, this is the way it must be.

Then there are the other two categories of border-crossers that are cause for even more concern due to their deliberate attempts to evade detection. The first I'll discuss is the "known gotaways."

According to the Department of Homeland Security (DHS) official website language, "Gotaways are defined as subjects at the Southwest Border who, after making an unlawful entry, are not turned back or apprehended, and are no longer being actively pursued by USBP agents."

As of late 2023, nearly two million known gotaways have been documented crossing the border but evading apprehension. These are the border-hoppers who aren't even downloading the laughably easy CBP One app, because they evidently believe it's advantageous, or easier yet, not to do so.

One example of the hundreds of thousands of known gotaways occurred on the night of August 5, 2023, when three men of Mexican descent waded across the Rio Grande in the middle of the night, holding their carbines at shoulder level to keep the guns clear of the muddy water. They were caught by drone camera technology, or else we never would have detected them. One carried a U.S.-style fully automatic M4 assault rifle (the same type our Navy SEALs used to kill Osama bin Laden) with armor-piercing ("green tip") ammo; another one carried an AK-47. All wore body armor and enough spare magazines to co-star in a John Wick film. Even the most blind members of the progressive Left, after looking at the images, can't easily write these *hombres* off as "good guys, just looking for a better life in America," unless of course, they were just looking for a public shooting range in the middle of the night to burn off some steam. Hell no, they were looking to rob, traffic, torture, or extort for profit. Why else would they risk sneaking across with those weapons? Criminals such as these are willing to murder others who get in their way; we know this, because we have the bodies to prove it.

They snuck into the United States without being caught, despite interdiction efforts after they were detected by Texas Ranger drones outfitted with thermal/night vision cameras. It was evident that these guys had done this many times before, by the way they used the terrain to coolly evade arrest when the Rangers tried to interdict them. A bigger group of armed men had been captured on drone video just a few weeks prior to this incident.

No doubt this happens tens of millions of times each year, up and down the border, from Brownsville to San Diego and everywhere in between. To explain this number, remember that many instances involve the same people crossing numerous times weekly if not daily. We just seldom have had proof, because only recently have we had drones and thermal technology available. Exactly what these marauders did while in America is unknown, but we can assume it *wasn't* preparing Easter baskets for homeless children or delivering meals on wheels to the elderly.

There is a somewhat happy ending to this story, however: On August 10, after nonstop surveillance of the area, two of the three border bandits were arrested when they were spotted recrossing the Rio Grande going back into Mexico. Canine units on the ground, combined with thermal vision technology from the air, led to their capture. Luckily, none of our guys were hurt. Both criminals were sentenced to five years in U.S. federal prison.

Notably, we learned that these two criminals were members of the Northeast Cartel. Of course, they denied everything, saying that they had been lost and hadn't known that they had crossed into the United States. Such excuses are, of course, laughable, but not when an anonymous U.S. spokesperson parroted these claims, telling American news sources: "They were under the impression they were still in Mexico."

This gaslighting quote highlights a major problem that will continually hamper our ability to make real progress on the border: Why do this administration and its cronies who head law enforcement agencies, such as the U.S. Department of Justice, refuse to call a spade a spade? That is what incenses me most and should incense all Americans. Until our leaders admit there is a problem, the problem will not be solved.

The Mayorkas-tenure spokesperson should have said something like "These criminal, armed trespassers said they were under the impression that they were still in Mexico, but, of course, we know that is complete BS. So, we will not stop until we gain all the intel we can possibly glean from these dangerous parasites before we put them in prison and go after their criminal comrades." But we heard no such talk. And until this administration leaves office, I'm afraid we never will.

From January 2021, when Biden assumed the helm, to the end of 2022, more than 1.32 million aliens entered the country illegally and undocumented. While the official number for 2023 has not been released yet, I expect it to be in the 650,000 range, bringing the total number of gotaways to over two million in just three years, from 2021 to 2023! A country cannot accept this many people in such a short time and not be permanently altered in some way.

To add insult to injury, in May of 2023, a leaked memo revealed that the administration had ordered a halt to the familial DNA testing of migrant children brought across the border. The policy had been installed by Trump when data indicated that a significant portion of children crossing the border were unrelated to the people who claimed to be their families. This loophole was exploited by the cartels to traffic these kids into the country. The familial DNA testing provided a means to combat this issue. Why the Biden administration would end this policy designed to protect children as well as American citizens is nothing less than baffling. It has declined to comment on its reasoning. I suspect it is at least in part due to the backlog that the rapid DNA tests could create when they want to avoid the Trump-like optics of immigrants being held in detention centers. Whatever the reasoning, cartels are wasting no time using the loophole to line their pockets as they game the system.

Finally, there are the nefarious, illegal immigrants who cross the border completely undetected. These are the ghosts we sense are coming over (or under, via tunnels) but don't see. Their numbers are likely just as many as the known gotaways, but we have no way of knowing exactly. I can tell you with certainty, however, that it is not an insignificant number, but that isn't the most alarming part. Rather, it's what these skilled, yet faceless, criminal aliens are up to.

These truly are the worst of the worst, the criminal aliens and terrorists who have something to hide—likely lengthy criminal records and backpacks full of guns and drugs, trucks packed with human slave cargo—or else they would be taking advantage of the administration's welcome mat, free drinks, and hotel rooms in an American city of their choosing. These are the people who must remain off all government databases, because their business depends on being able to hop back and forth across the border anonymously to deliver their sinister wares.

This is perhaps the scariest result of unsecured borders: We don't know who's coming in, because these gotaways and unknowns have no intentions of playing by any rules or obeying any laws. They are in the business of breaking laws, and that lends them their advantage. They will continue to operate covertly until drastic, no-tolerance laws, state-of-the-art border security, and relentless enforcement are adopted by America's leaders and implemented on our borders and everywhere else these criminals slither.

If you don't think some include terrorists, you might be naive to reality and suffering from the same failure of imagination that this country suffered leading up to the despicable attacks of 9/11. Each month, officials are encountering an ever-growing number of people who are on the terrorist watch list. And we also know that CBP is encountering aliens from as many as 170 countries in the world, many of which are known adversaries of the United States. If anyone thinks all of the refugees from Afghanistan who made their way onto military aircraft and were delivered to America during the administration's flawed and chaotic pullout from the country were vetted, they had better think again! There's a reason why the FBI, to this day, is still scrambling to find many of them within the United States.

Still, the real question is, *How many terrorists are we not encountering at our borders?* With the rising numbers of illegal migrants who are encountered and who are on the terrorist watch list, isn't it common sense to believe that significant terrorist threats are entering but are not being encountered? This is a game of Russian roulette that our own government is forcing us to play.

The gotaways and the undetected are the worst type of "immigrants" we can have, as they can move around covertly, committing crimes if they wish and then hopping back over the border when they feel the heat on their tails. If they do make money in America, it cannot be taxed. If they kill someone, we have no fingerprint or biological data to be matched to crime scene evidence or any trace of their existence except for the carnage they caused while here.

Meanwhile, the Biden administration is turning a blind eye to this obvious problem. They do not even like to talk about it, but when pressed, they consistently give numbers much lower than Border Patrol experts on the border estimate.

In 2022, CBP made 12,028 arrests of criminal aliens. Most were simply turned away, without thorough vetting or prosecution. And do you know what these people did? Many of them laughed at the stupid American policies and simply tried again. Many of them succeeded in entering over time. It's a game of numbers that we are losing. The fact is our government has no idea how many terrorists are in our country. And it is showing virtually no signs of caring.

If we are to solve this problem, certainly we must have secure borders and tough policy, but we also must have a thorough and competent vetting system in place. We must toughen our borders and strengthen our entire immigration system right now. In the chapters ahead, I'll tell how.

CHAPTER SIX

TCOs and Fentanyl, the Cartels' New Cash Cow

Fentanyl overdoses become No. 1 cause of death among U.S. adults, ages 18–45: "A National Emergency."

—Fox News headline, December 16, 2021

Still steaming with sweat from an epic win against crosstown rivals, 17-year-old Chris removed his shoulder pads and waded through throngs of people to the brick wall separating the field from the grandstands. It was a post-game tradition to say hello to his mom and dad, and he certainly wasn't going to break it after the last home game he'd ever play. As a defensive starter, Chris was a pretty darn good high-school football player, but Arizona is a hotbed for great players, and at 5 feet 9, 175 pounds, he was under no illusion that football would remain a part of his life after graduation. He'd been accepted to Arizona State University on a partial academic scholarship. He planned to earn a business degree, and he hoped to start a company someday.

But right then, on that cool desert night in Tucson, he had other things on his mind.

Under the waning glare of the Friday night lights, Chris hugged his parents and then found his girlfriend of two years—whom we'll call Kate—and told her he'd see her soon at the party. From there, he quickly regrouped with his teammates to shower and change before stopping to score some booze on their way to the bash. The win meant the team had made the district playoffs, and they were going to celebrate as only high-school seniors knew how.

By 10 p.m., the party was hopping, with 16- to 20-year-old kids in the house, on the back deck surrounding the keg, and spilling into the backyard after having been vacated from the front porch when a neighbor threatened to call the police due to excessive noise. It was sometime around 11:30 when one of Chris' non-football-playing friends invited him into a bathroom, saying he had "a special surprise for the man who ran back an interception for a touchdown."

Chris had tried cocaine once before, and so he was not entirely surprised when the friend used a credit card to cut out two big white lines on the tile countertop. The boys sniffed one line each, and after fist bumping, they returned to the party, where Chris found Kate talking to a group of her friends in the living room.

Six minutes later, Chris crumpled to the carpet, where he soon lost consciousness. Meanwhile, outside, the friend who had given Chris the coke was also unconscious, but the others just thought he had gotten too drunk, and they were laughing, urging him to puke.

Kate, however, knew better. She had seen Chris drunk several times, but never like this. He had been fine just a few minutes earlier. She began yelling at Chris to snap out of it, but there was no response. Her first thought was that he'd had a heart attack, so she began yelling at Chris' friends and teammates—anyone—to help. They responded admirably by hurriedly carrying Chris to her car. Thinking it would be quicker to drive to the hospital than to wait for an ambulance, she sped away with one of his friends holding Chris in the backseat while she dialed 911. Next she called his parents as she frantically drove. But moments after arriving at the ER, and before doctors had time to find out that Chris had overdosed on fentanyl, so they could administer naloxone, the 17-year-old, 3.75-GPA high-school student who was, by most measures, a typical, if not great, American young man, was dead.

As you can imagine, Chris' parents—who had watched him play football just a few hours earlier—were in complete shock. As the hours and days dragged by, their shock morphed to sadness, then to confusion, and then mostly to anger as they searched for answers.

As a thorough investigation and a toxicology report would confirm a couple weeks later, Chris, like nearly 70,000 other Americans in 2021, died from an accidental overdose of fentanyl. The cocaine had been laced with it. The friend who had given it to him survived; neither had known what they were ingesting. In testimony later, the friend said he had purchased the cocaine that evening from a low-level drug-dealer classmate whom everyone knew. When police threatened the juvenile dealer with jail time and questioned him in the presence of his upper-middle-class parents, he said he had bought the stuff from a "Mexican cartel dude" whom he heard crossed the border at will and "who always has cheap cocaine, weed, and pills" to sell.

Although it was in his best interest to name this person to save himself from more charges, the high-school dealer was adamant that he didn't know the source's name—and the detectives believed him. Why did they believe him? Because he described the guy as a "smaller Mexican dude who always carries a gun with gray duct tape around its grip," and one who "had a creepy tattoo of a cross and a dove under his jawbone." The agents knew cartel drug traffickers are too cagey to give out their real names, but they'd had heard this description in an APB (all-points bulletin) from a trafficking victim-turned-informant, a 15-year-old Mexican immigrant named Maria.

TRANSNATIONAL CRIME ORGANIZATIONS AND THE MEXICAN CARTELS

There is ample information on the world's cartels and the history of drug smuggling, so I'm not going to give a historic account here. (If you are fascinated by this stuff, I suggest listening to *The Shawn Ryan Podcast*, episode No. 38, wherein former Navy SEAL Ryan interviews Roger Reaves, a convicted American drug smuggler for Pablo Escobar. The stories this old guy tells are incredible! Having done 30 years in federal prison, he's immune from prosecution of the crimes for which he was tried, and so his stories may be true.) But before we get into specific Mexican cartels that now dominate the illicit drug industry, I'll quickly summarize how they came into power.

In the 1970s, Pablo Escobar's Medellín Cartel and the lower-profile, but more powerful, Cali Cartel (both based in

Colombia) came into great power after learning how much money first-world people (Americans and others) would pay for cocaine and how much easier and profitable it was to smuggle than bulky marijuana. Both cartels learned how to smuggle it in large quantities—mainly via Florida and the Gulf Coast for the Medellín cartel—so that in the 1980s, Escobar was purported to make $60 million per day! (At his peak, Escobar was one of the world's richest men, having amassed a fortune estimated at $30 billion.)

However, when the crack epidemic and accompanying inner-city crime wave became intolerable to the American people, President Ronald Reagan declared the U.S. war on drugs; he promoted zero-tolerance trafficking policies, relentless surveillance, interdiction, and hopelessly long prison sentences and generally began making life very tough for smugglers due to the fact that the Gulf's coastline was highly guarded with manpower, technology, and surveillance of incoming planes and ships. In 1993, Escobar was finally killed in his own country by a Colombian paramilitary unit. Now free from Escobar's psychopathic, deadly reign of terror for which he was labeled a "narco-terrorist" by world governments, authorities could focus their efforts on the savvy leaders of the Cali Cartel, eventually forcing them on the run and finally arresting them in 1995.

It was at this time that the Colombian cartel influence was severely diminished because with the DEA now privy to the Colombians' smuggling MOs, the Colombia cartel masterminds were forced to rely on middlemen in Mexico to consistently traffic its illicit goods into the United States. It chose Mexican cartels for three reasons. First was of course Mexico's geopolitical positioning as America's neighbors; a pipeline from Central

America to the United States. Second, organized criminal organizations looking for large scale cash opportunities were emerging. And third, Mexico's leadership was known to be open to bribes. You don't have to obtain a degree from Wharton to recognize a better business model when you see one. Why pay your guys to smuggle when you can pay someone else to do it?

So, in the mid- to late-1990s, various Mexican cartels, such as the Gulf Cartel, the Tijuana Cartel, and others, began filling the tremendous drug business vacuum created by the absence of the Colombians. This shift allowed Mexican cartels to gain more power and revenue, which begat more power and more revenue. In essence, the demise of the Colombian cartels allowed Mexican cartels to get a stranglehold on the North American drug market.

By the 2000s, the Mexican cartels naturally assumed an even larger role in the drug trade. Not only did they traffic cocaine from Colombia, but they also began diversifying their operations to include methamphetamine, MDMA, heroin, and other opioids.

In 2006, Mexican president Felipe Calderon mobilized nearly 50,000 troops and federal police to combat the cartels. (Unfortunately, a startling number of these troops defected to the cartels, along with their weapons and training.) Then, in 2008, with passage of the Mérida Initiative, the United States partnered with Mexico to combat the cartels with financial aid, intelligence resources, and training.

While the partnership certainly took a toll on several major cartels at the time, it had two unintended consequences: First mobilizing the military increased the militarization of the cartels, who knew they also must ramp up their weapons, intelligence, and training if they were to survive. Second, the killing of leaders often led to violent fragmentation of cartels, which led to a greater number of smaller groups vying for power through violence.

By 2010, several of Mexico's cartels became the world's preeminent drug traffickers and general instigators of North American violence. Several still are. But before we focus on Mexican cartels who, pathetically, are considered the southern gatekeepers of the United States–Mexico border, let's first expand our focus to all of the major transnational criminal organizations, as the DEA refers to them, that influence crime in America.

Colombian TCOs

Roughly 90 percent of all cocaine in the United States originates from Colombia before most is smuggled into the United States by Mexican TCOs. Most Colombian TCOs are smaller spinoffs of the Revolutionary Armed Forces of Colombia, or FARC. DEA analysis indicates that Colombian TCOs generate as much as $10 billion each year in drug-based revenue.

The DEA says the Gulf Clan (aka Los Urabeños, aka Clan del Golfo, aka Clan Úsuga) "is the most significant Colombian TCO with an impact on the U.S. drug market."

Dominican TCOs

With New York City as their hub, Dominican TCOs dominate the cocaine and heroin distribution in the Northeastern corridor of the United States, according to the DEA's 2020 National Drug Threat Assessment. While they are smaller than the major Mexican cartels in scope, revenue, and influence, the Dominican TCOs are not to be underestimated.

Asian TCOs

Asian TCOs are the most prolific traffickers of MDMA, though they also profit from marijuana, cocaine, heroin, and other drugs. Asian TCOs often smuggle MDMA through Canada. Recently, they have been buying properties and growing marijuana in grow houses in the interior United States for both the legal and illegal markets. Asian TCOs frequently serve as money-laundering agents to many other TCOs, including those from Mexico, due to their access to Hong Kong and Taiwan, where they can easily set up shell companies.

Mexican TCOs

Mexican TCOs serve as the gatekeepers for most of the illegal drug, firearm, and human trafficking across the United States' southwest border. As of 2023, the most powerful, active cartels include:

- **Sinaloa Cartel.** Likely the most prominent in Mexico, the Sinaloa Cartel was led by the infamous Joaquín "El Chapo" Guzmán until his capture in 2016. It operates in many states across Mexico, including Sinaloa, Sonora, Nayarit, and others. It is the largest cartel in terms of revenue—mostly derived from the drug trade—and therefore likely the most powerful. It is also known to have significant international reach, and it considers the U.S. cities of Los Angeles, Denver, Phoenix, Atlanta, and others as its distribution turf. Like nearly all of the cartels that seize upon any income stream they can, the Sinaloa specializes in drug trafficking, drug production, human trafficking, money laundering, oil theft, arms trafficking, extortion, protection rackets, kidnapping, and even some

legitimate businesses. Like all of the other cartels, it benefits from lax border security, favorable immigration laws,
progressive politics, America's vast drug market, corruption of government officials, and U.S.-imported weapons.
It has a thorough knowledge of America's laws and how
to use the system against itself. It is one of two major
suppliers of fentanyl in the United States, most of which
it gets from China. However, it is now producing its own
fentanyl in clandestine laboratories.

- **Jalisco New Generation Cartel (CJNG).** On the rise
since 2010, CJNG has gained significant power. As of
2020, it is the second most powerful in terms of revenue, but it is regarded as the most dangerous due to its
highly militaristic operations and ruthless *sicarios* and hit
teams. It operates primarily in the state of Jalisco but has
expanded operations into other states. It is now thought
to have a presence in at least 28 U.S. states. CJNG is the
other major fentanyl-trafficking organization.

- **Beltran Leyva Organization.** Originally allied with the
Sinaloa Cartel, this group, which is named after its leader,
split off in 2008 and has been involved in violent conflicts
with its former allies. It operates in several states, including Sinaloa, Guerrero, Morelos, and Mexico State. Some
reports rank it as the third most powerful cartel.

- **Gulf Cartel.** This is one of the oldest cartels, based in
the border region near Texas, particularly in Tamaulipas
State. It was an original trafficking partner of the Cali
Cartel of Colombia. The Gulf Cartel has seen its power
wane in recent years due to internal splits, infighting, and
pressure from other cartels.

- **Zetas Cartel.** Once the armed wing of the Gulf Cartel consisting of Mexican special forces soldiers, Los Zetas split from their former employers and became known for ruthless violence. The main base of operations is in the northeastern states of Tamaulipas, Nuevo León, and Coahuila.
- **Juarez Cartel.** Based in Ciudad Juárez, Chihuahua, near the border with Texas, and one of the oldest, this cartel has been involved in a bloody turf war with the Sinaloa Cartel.
- **Tijuana Cartel.** Also known as the Arellano Felix Organization, this gang of drug-running *banditos* operates in the border region near California but has lost much of its power in recent years due to pressure from rival cartels and law enforcement.
- **Cartel de Santa Rosa de Lima.** Based in Mexico's Guanajuato State, in the past this group was primarily focused on fuel theft. It has been in a violent conflict with the CJNG.
- **Los Rojas.** This smaller, but very violent, cartel was founded in 2009 when some militant members of the Mexican navy split off from the Beltran Leyva Cartel. Its primary business is trafficking drugs into the United States.

EVER-EVOLVING CARTEL TACTICS AND THE FENTANYL THREAT

As I've underscored in previous chapters, there are many serious problems created by leaving our borders unsecured and canceling proven policies. But the one that scares me most, due to its risk of destroying the lives of everyday Americans, is the Mexican cartel element, whose illicit goods, members, and associates can now basically flow between the two countries at will. As the good people of Mexico know all too well, once any of these organizations gets a foothold in a community, state, or, God forbid, a government, it is extremely tough to eliminate them due to their clandestine, loosely structured nature and overall knowledge of their trade.

In the past, however, the leaders of Mexican cartels didn't *want* to operate in America. The risk of falling onto the radar of superior U.S. law enforcement and intelligence agencies wasn't worth the reward when they could simply contract their trafficking to criminal elements, mafia, and gangs already in the United States.

But evidently, now some of the cartels are realizing they might be leaving money on the table when it's so easy to scoot across the border and handle their business for themselves. The Texas Ranger drone images (from August 2023) of three armed cartel members sneaking across the border prove it, not that we didn't already know it. But these days, crossing the border is much easier than swimming across the Rio Grande or climbing a fence.

Now, all a cartel must do is recruit a person, preferably a youngish-looking one with a clean record (many cartel *sicarios* are juveniles anyway), have that person download the CBP One app, and claim they are an unaccompanied minor, and bingo, they are in. Then they are free to do what they wish. Remember that the Biden administration nixed the requirement of even administering routine background checks to alien minors! (Since fiscal year 2021, there have been roughly 400,000 unaccompanied minors encountered while crossing the border. A *New York Times* study suggested that 85,000 of these kids, many of whom are exploited during the travel process, have disappeared from the government's radar.) For the gang-banging minors among them, if they don't get caught committing a crime while in America, they can roam across the country like any citizen, delivering drugs and/ or providing intel to their leaders back in Mexico. And if they do get caught, well, the cartel will just hire more.

The Internet, specifically social apps, has made covert international communication a snap. Meanwhile, cash apps, and especially cryptocurrency, have only complicated the government's ability to monitor their money transfers and laundering.

Rest assured, these criminal syndicates are into everything that can turn a buck—including the most heinous acts of humanity, such as kidnapping, human trafficking (yes, this mostly means kidnapping and selling minors for sex to pedophiles); inundating the streets, suburbs, and schools with fentanyl; extorting people for cash; and murdering whenever it suits them.

According to an official DEA press release issued on May 5, 2023:

> Operation Last Mile comprised 1,436 investigations
> conducted from May 1, 2022, through May 1, 2023, in
> collaboration with federal, state, and local law enforcement
> partners, and resulted in 3,337 arrests and the seizure
> of nearly 44 million fentanyl pills, more than 6,500
> pounds of fentanyl powder, more than 91,000 pounds of
> methamphetamine, 8,497 firearms, and more than $100
> million. The fentanyl powder and pill seizures equate to
> nearly 193 million deadly doses of fentanyl removed from
> communities across the United States, which have prevented
> countless potential drug poisoning deaths. Among these

investigations, more than 1,100 cases involved social media
applications and encrypted communications platforms,
including Facebook, Instagram, TikTok, Snapchat, WhatsApp,
Telegram, Signal, Wire, and Wickr.

These numbers should scare the ever-living hell out of any parent whose children are or will be navigating the Wild West world of social media and peer pressures in which we now live. Especially scary is fentanyl, where one mistake caused by curiosity can snuff out a young life with the unforgiving efficiency of a Victor mousetrap.

One question I often get is: *Why would drug traffickers and dealers sell fentanyl when it could kill their own clientele??*

The answer is that fentanyl makes better business sense to them. In terms of its weight-to-value ratio, it is so much more potent for its size and weight, and therefore easier to smuggle in bulk than cocaine, cannabis, or other opioids. It's also cheaper to make, as there are no crops involved—only crude labs and buyable chemicals. No land, water, fertilizer, or farm labor is required.

Discounting the fact that many junkies desire fentanyl for its potency (it's 50 to 100 times more potent than morphine), dealers sometimes lace other drugs with fentanyl to give the illusion that their drugs are very pure and/or potent. It's also very addictive, which, in theory, should increase business. The problem is, when users don't know what they are taking, and they have no tolerance built up for fentanyl, even a minuscule amount can kill them. In fact, fentanyl was responsible for 77 percent of juvenile overdose deaths in 2021.[1]

The answer is fentanyl is so lucrative that the cartels are willing to sacrifice a portion of its clientele for it.

Fentanyl is especially scary when you realize that any cartel member (or American drug dealer, for that matter) with a particularly sinister bent can play to citizens' addictions and intentionally kill them—all while making money. It is especially sinister to sell this stuff to unwitting, temptation-susceptible teenagers who may just be experimenting with drugs in high school or college as they try to find their way.

According to numerous sources, including Families Against Fentanyl, fentanyl poisoning is the number 1 cause of death of Americans aged 18 to 45. I was also surprised at the number of toddlers killed by fentanyl poisoning. Evidently, the drug is so potent that if a baby or toddler gets it on their hands and rubs them in their mouth, they can die. According to official statistics, it happens more times than most of us can fathom.

Certainly, any market requires a buyer and a seller, and America has plenty of buyers, to be sure. But there's a reason I'm blaming the fentanyl crisis on the Mexican cartels and the Chinese producers: I'm doing so because that's where the fentanyl is coming from. In the recent past, fentanyl would get to Mexico via China, but these days, Chinese makers have taught the elicit recipe to cartels, who make it at will, smuggle it over the border, and sell it to our people.

The Sinaloa Cartel specifically has "demonstrated ability to run clandestine fentanyl synthesis labs in Sinaloa Cartel dominant areas in Mexico," according to the 2020 National Drug Threat Assessment released by the DEA. According to U.S. Border Patrol Chief Jason Owens, fentanyl seizures were up 175 percent in 2023, compared to 2022.

Now don't get me wrong—I believe that anyone of proper age and sound mind who willingly takes an illegal drug owns most of the responsibility for doing so. But in this case, if it weren't for the cartels' purposeful distribution of fentanyl, it wouldn't be as much of a problem. According to a summary of a December 2022 DEA press release, the Sinaloa and Jalisco Cartels are responsible for much of the fentanyl and methamphetamine that is killing Americans.[2]

(It's possible that even the cartels have become sensitive to all the negative publicity they've been receiving over fentanyl. In mid-2023, banners hung over overpasses, supposedly placed by the Sinaloa cartel, claimed to be cracking down on any cartel member affiliated with the deadly drug. To this, I'd say: Take any cartel "public service" message with a grain of salt, as they have become good at the propaganda game over the years.)

I hate to use the term "lucky" here, but lucky for us, the cartels—at least now—are only in the business of making money; their tactics are used to minimize and/or eliminate governmental interference in their profit-making operations. They are not political groups looking to overturn governments or induce social chaos, even though they do so as a byproduct of their trade.

But can you imagine if their goal were to overthrow governments or to simply promote terror via death and destruction with such a weapon? Hmmm, it would almost be like another group of radical people whom we know all too well from the events of 9/11.

Can you imagine if a true terrorist organization were to get hold of kilos of fentanyl for the sole purpose of lacing our food and beverages with it? They can get large quantities of the drug anytime from Chinese or Mexican distributors. And, as we know, plenty of those on the terrorist watch list have been caught at the border. So, it seems to me that the best way we can stop future large-scale fentanyl terror is by budgeting giant figures for intel (both via boots on the ground and technology-based counter-terrorism equipment), comprehensive immigrant-vetting systems, and tightening our borders and immigration policy. These measures require the vote of Congress and the signature of a president who agrees.

But it's not just fentanyl that keeps me up at night.

You might not know this, but since 1970, with the passage of the Bank Secrecy Act, which was ramped up in 1986 and yet again by the passage of the Patriot Act in 2001, all of the major American financial institutions have entire divisions that are mandated to help the federal government identify crime via transactional banking patterns. For the last 40 years or so, the primary crimes these analysts have searched for have been money-laundering operations that were most often set up by criminal organizations in the business of trafficking drugs. Indeed, the cartels have become the world's foremost experts in money laundering. But in the last several years, there has been a shift: Now the banks' anti-money-laundering divisions have subdivisions that are focused on human trafficking.

Expert analysis of an account with many debit cards connected to it, and whose cardholders receive consistent, smaller amounts from the master account that are then withdrawn immediately after they are deposited, for example, can be indicative of human trafficking patterns. How many human trafficking rings the big banks have uncovered in the last couple years would be shocking to most Americans.

Around 200,000 instances of human trafficking are reported each year, and the trend is increasing annually. About one in five of these instances involves a minor. At the same time, it's estimated that cartels make as much as $6 billion profit just from trafficking immigrants across the border. Many of them, such as Maria in our story, wind up as sex slaves.

While an unacceptable amount of this sickening variety of crime is American-on-American, a significant portion of it is committed by the cartels, who specialize in preying on vulnerable people.

But it's not just fentanyl and human trafficking that I'm worried about. It's crime in general—both violent and nonviolent—that has the most potential to bring America as we know it to its knees over the long haul. Not only does crime affect people's daily lives, but it also destroys our economy and places untenable pressure upon our nation's resources. It does so by raising insurance, legal, penal, and healthcare costs—taxes—for everyone.

The bottom line is the cartels are in the business of making money via crime. It's what they do. Since the early 2000s, you haven't been able to take a vacation in otherwise lovely Mexico without worrying about getting killed, your kids being kidnapped, and your parents being extorted for their last cent if they are to see you again. But now some of these nightmares are happening within America's own borders, and our government should be ashamed.

CHAPTER SEVEN

Redefining the Cartels

The hacked-up remains of 27 people have been found in several graves in the northern Mexican border town of Reynosa, just south of McAllen, Texas.

—*Border Report* Tweet, July 20, 2023

I n the past, Mexican cartels operated in the United States primarily through sophisticated (and unsophisticated) distribution networks that brought humans, illegal drugs, and other contraband into the country. These networks span cities, states, and regions and have historically involved U.S.-based gangs who can handle street-level distribution, allowing the cartels to minimize their direct exposure while maintaining control over the supply chain. However, as border restrictions ease, cartels can pass their goods to other cartel members who have entered the country and set up shop.

To be sure, however, cartels still operate via corruption and bribery. Just as in Mexico, cartels attempt to corrupt U.S. officials, though without nearly as much success. They commonly try to bribe Border Patrol agents, local police, or other officials to turn a blind eye to their activities. Of course, one of the reasons for their power and effectiveness is the vast amounts of money they make.

It's reported that the infamous former leader of the Sinaloa Cartel, El Chapo, accumulated a personal fortune somewhere around $12 billion. This enabled him to pay security guards $2.5 million plus another $5 million for construction of an underground tunnel—a drop in his proverbial bucket—to allow his escape from Altiplano Federal Penitentiary in Almoloya de Juárez, Mexico, on July 15, 2015. The net worth of the Sinaloa Cartel is likely similar to the Medellín Cartel's past $30 billion fortune, a figure that would have put it solidly on *Forbes'* list of the 500 richest businesses today.

This kind of money allows more than bribing jailers and politicians; it can buy submarines, fleets of go-fast boats, thermal imaging drones, computer technology, countersurveillance teams, 18-wheelers, armies of men, laboratories, 747s—you name it. No doubt, the 1,500-foot-long, air-conditioned tunnel the cartel built under the border between Tijuana and San Diego cost it a mint, but what is certain is that it paid off in spades. The point is that the cartels have almost unlimited money to spend on their illicit craft, so by no means do I think our government's job of establishing operational control will ever be easy. But for starters, we all must agree that there is a problem, and that's where I have a problem with the Biden administration's "The border is secure" nonsense.

Right now, there is an interesting, if not disingenuous, debate going on among legislators in Congress as I write this.

THEY ARE AMONG US

Some, including the cartels themselves, claim that Mexican cartels only have "clients" in the United States, that include couriers, drug dealers, hitmen, and others, whom they contract to distribute their drugs, rather than actual salaried members of the cartel living in the United States. Many progressive leaders in the United States, especially those who promote open borders, agree with them. They claim that the cartels know they should keep a low profile in America, where their bribery and corruption schemes aren't nearly as effective. But recent findings suggest otherwise.

According to a February 2023 NewsNation article, "More than 300 people in the United States have been charged or arrested for criminal activity directly linked to Mexican drug cartels. . . ."[1]

On November 17, 2022, Ismael Salas Navarro pleaded guilty in a Houston court for conspiracy to distribute two kilos of methamphetamine. He was ensnared by a law enforcement operation in which officers were surveilling members of the Gulf Cartel. Navarro, who was operating out of a house in a Houston suburb, was sentenced to 135 months in federal prison.

Each year, there are hundreds of instances wherein known cartel members are arrested for committing crimes in the United States—and they are not just in border towns and border states. In late 2022, for example, 22 active members of the Sinaloa cartel were arrested for trafficking fentanyl and other drugs, not in San Diego, Dallas, or Phoenix, but all the way up in Big Sky, Montana!

There have been arrests everywhere, including in big cities and small towns, indicating that cartels are evolving and finding undersupplied markets.

Certainly, it's in the best interests of U.S.-based cartel members to keep a low profile and not garner the attention of U.S. law enforcement, so there's no telling how many live and operate in the states who haven't been caught. Nevertheless, one thing is for sure: The number is increasing as border security and enforcement decrease. I don't mean to frighten you, but dangerous cartel members and their deadly drugs are everywhere among us.

Consider this: In August 2023, a Brazilian ex-police officer convicted of killing and torturing 11 people, including children, was found in Rye, New Hampshire. This should tell us something: Brazil contains some of the most remote places on the planet. Hell, there are tribes there who have never been contacted by the outside world. Nearby Panama and the Darien Gap are about as wild as Mother Earth gets, not to mention the remote hills of Old Mexico, where Pancho Villa eluded the U.S. Army indefinitely. Nope, Antonio Jose De Abreu Vidal Filho chose to hide in jolly old Rye, New Hampshire. Why? Likely because it was so easy to get there, and once he got there, he knew he could use America's pro-immigrant laws to his advantage. With the help of INTERPOL, he was finally caught. Thank heavens for that, but how many more dangerous criminal aliens are hiding among us?

My sympathies go out to the Mexican people who have been bullied by the cartels for as long as most living folks can remember. Can you imagine trying to carve out an honest living as a citizen of Mexico? I truly feel sorry for those people, who must endure the constant threat of cartel violence while trying to raise a family amid a stifling economy and live in peace. I do not envy them.

On August 17, 2023, Mexican authorities found the burned, tortured, and decapitated remains of four youths who were kidnapped by cartel members at a festival in the city of Lagos de Moreno. A video was found in which the kids were filmed while alive, as the fifth youth—a best friend of the others—was forced to bludgeon the others to death with a brick and then cut their heads off. Crimes like this should be enough for the Mexican and the U.S. governments to declare war on these money-hungry, honorless animals and work together to exterminate them and stamp out their nests.

REDEFINING THE CARTELS: CALLING THEM WHAT THEY ARE

No matter how much some nationalist hawks call for isolationism, we cannot get around the fact that Mexico and the United States are inextricably linked by geography, multinational families, trade, business, shared interests, religion, and, to some extent, culture. This interdependence requires that both countries work closely together, beyond the area of trade, to institute an effective and coordinated strategy to diminish the shared threat that the Mexican drug cartels present to both countries' national and economic security.

With a change in strategy and commitment to work together, I believe Mexico can improve its dismal security situation. Meanwhile, if Mexican officials can prove their sincere commitment to the effort, the United States must provide greater assistance. However, after learning from some of the past failures when going after the cartels, I've come around to newer thinking.

You see, I used to think that the cartel influence—especially when it was more limited to Mexico—should not be called an insurgency; therefore, I felt it should be dealt with not by the Mexican and U.S. militaries that traditionally have not been great at pure law enforcement duties. Rather, I felt that the United States should prioritize its assistance through the Mérida Initiative on strengthening Mexico's law enforcement institutions. I viewed this as a more holistic approach, one that would expand Mérida to serve as an effective regional tool in disrupting illicit drug trafficking in the Central American and Caribbean regions.

Now, however, as time has passed, and Mexico's and America's policies and actions toward the cartels have allowed them to flourish, I am rethinking strategies.

The fact is, local police units do not have the scope, tools, resolve, or sheer manpower necessary to combat the more powerful cartels in an efficient way; what's more, they tend to be much more vulnerable to corruption and bribes. Mexican cartels also tend to be much better armed than local police, but they aren't going to outgun our boys in combat boots.

I believe the United States needs to call cartels what they have become: terrorists. Plain and simple, they are terrorists in every sense of the word; they are a clear and present threat to our national security. They are not even hiding it anymore. It's like a Trojan horse with the invaders riding on top of it rather than in it. And the enablers of this invasion are our very own president, his cabinet, and members of Congress who support open borders.

Even Mayorkas' Deputy Homeland Security Secretary John Tien, a 24-year Army vet, said as much in May of 2023. "The way al Qaeda operates is very similar to the way the cartels operate," he said. But there are several differences other than the obvious. The cartels are larger, they have more capability and they are already operating in our homeland as *domestic* terrorists. By redefining the cartels as terrorists, the U.S. government can invoke special powers to wage war against them wherever, however, and whenever they pop up.

After 20 years in Afghanistan, U.S. armed forces have become proficient at gaining the trust of the locals and rooting out terrorists wherever they thrive, even in nontraditional battlefields such as urban housing. We've learned to pay informants, just like the cartels do, while employing every method of intelligence-gathering technology that we are legally able to employ against foreign nationals who are bent on harming us. We must collectively come to the realization that our southern border may present as large of a security threat as any from Yemen or Somalia. I believe it's many times greater.

While we cannot overtly conduct war on Mexican soil without Mexico's express permission, we can wage war upon terrorists whose feet are on American soil. It's going to take a concerted effort by the CBP, DHS, ICE, the DEA, the CIA, and all other available agencies and resources to pull it off. Additionally, we must work with the Mexican government to embolden its military leaders, just as we must embolden our own to take hard stances against this terrorism, even if some of the resulting headlines won't be pretty. The Mexican people must be supplied with information to discern whether election candidates, all the way up to the presidential election, are puppets of the cartels. We must counter the cartels' propaganda and public relations campaigns with those of our own. We cannot be afraid to fight fire with fire.

The sad truth is that Mexico is a giant country that has every resource: It has gold, oil, minerals, lithium, limitless water, beaches, mountains, rain forests, high deserts, rich tradition, agriculture, infinite tourism possibilities, good colleges, great food, rich cities, wonderful small towns, and great hardworking people. It's an absolute shame that its government cannot get a grip on the cartels that hold it back from being a dominant force on the world stage as well as a formidable U.S. ally and trading partner. But no other country, including the United States, can do it all for them.

The Mexican people must say *"No mas"* and demand that their government wage all-out war on the cartels. The biggest obstacle, of course, is that it's estimated that the cartels represent Mexico's fifth-largest employer! Destroying the cartels would erase around 175,000 jobs. So, the first thing Mexico needs to do is spur its economy so that more jobs can be available. That is more easily said than done, I get it, but it's got to happen. Next, it must clean its own house by ousting corrupt government officials. It will be an arduous task, and it won't come without the blood of some innocent people being spilled, and it will get worse before it gets better. But until the cartels are destroyed, or at least reduced to second-tier dope peddlers, Mexicans will continue to be hostages in their own land. Until then, America cannot be the best it can be either.

But for now, what we can do is tighten our borders and officially classify the cartels as terrorists to invoke our military where needed. Meanwhile—as I'll outline in the chapters ahead—we should create incentives for the Mexican government and its people to . . . get cracking.

CHAPTER EIGHT

Why Past Attempts at Combating the Cartels Have Failed

Violence cannot be confronted with violence.

—Mexican President Andres Manuel López Obrador,
when he doubled down on his ineffective
"hugs, not bullets" strategy to defeat the cartels

For as much as I've railed against the Biden administration for its vapid policies, and to a lesser extent, the Mexican government, I honestly do not believe anyone, except the cartels themselves, a few corrupt Mexican politicians, and perhaps the drug dealers who are supplied by them, wants to see the cartels flourish. Most people just want to live in peace.

Mexico alone has experienced more than 360,000 cartel-affiliated homicides since 2006. While many of those victims have included politicians, police, and journalists—148 journalists were slain from 2000 to 2022—the majority have been innocent people of Mexico who have somehow crossed paths with these thugs.[1]

So, how is it that these despised TCOs who sow incalculable chaos and death in their own country not only survive among its populace but thrive? It's due to the cartels' money and influence, and the opportunities they provide Mexico's desperate people.

Over the decades, beginning on a large, federal scale with the Reagan administration, the United States has spent billions of dollars and countless man hours and precious lives trying to cut the cartels down at their roots when and where we have been politically able to do so. And there have been many successes, to be sure.

In 2006, Cali Cartel founding brothers Gilberto Rodríguez Orejuela and Miguel Rodríguez Orejuela were extradited to prison in the United States. Gilberto died there. You no doubt recall the infamous arrest, imprisonment, tunnel escape, and re-arrest and extradition of Sinaloa Cartel boss Joaquín "El Chapo" Guzmán Loera. He's sitting in Colorado's ADX Florence prison, called "the Alcatraz of the Rockies," right now, we hope not having a ton of fun. (In fact, in early 2023, via his lawyers, he sent the equivalent of an SOS to President Obrador asking for extradition back to Mexico due to alleged "physical torment.") One of his sons, Ovidio Guzmán, was caught in January of 2023 by Mexican security forces.

For a very recent example of another U.S. victory, in mid-August of 2023, U.S. marshals executed an arrest warrant for Adan Salazar Zamorano, aka "Don Adan," the leader of the "Los Salazar" cell of the Sinaloa Cartel. He was captured and then extradited by the Mexican government to the United States, where he is now in prison for trafficking cocaine and for the murders of nine Americans, including women and children, whose bodies were savagely burned. You probably remember the LeBarón and Langford families massacre that involved an innocent group of Latter-Day Saints who were headed to a small community called La Mora just across the border from Douglas, Arizona, in 2019. It was senseless and shockingly brutal, but the capture of Don Adan was also very revealing: When the United States is determined to go after cartel leadership—and puts enough political pressure on Mexico to give it rein—our military units are capable of hunting down these terrorists on their own turf and extraditing them to justice on ours. But seldom is the United States allowed to do so.

I could go on with hundreds of more names who have been taken down over the years, and that's the point. It seems that no matter how many cartel members we arrest, without the full cooperation of the Mexican government and winning the hearts of its weary people, stamping out the cartels in Mexico is like trying to wipe out a colony of ants: There is a nearly endless supply of worker ants that will replace those who are ousted. If the queen is killed, another one will take its place. If you blow up the whole ant hill, survivors will go underground, only to resurface as several more colonies down the road.

But before we get into specifics on why efforts to dismantle the cartels haven't worked, let's first take a broader look into some of the root causes of crime in general.

POVERTY: THE ROOT CAUSE OF CRIME

In just about every instance in the modern world, the root cause of crime is poverty. It's as simple as that. Certainly, drug use alone contributes to crime as does pure greed, but poverty is also a big reason why people use drugs to momentarily escape their dire reality. (Sure, you can argue that plenty of middle-class and even very wealthy people use drugs, but these people aren't often those who are out robbing, stealing, and killing for their fix.) It's obvious in America, although plenty of Americans don't realize that all of Mexico is a giant market for drugs on its own. The point is, find the places with the highest poverty, and you'll generally find the most crime, as well.

In Mexico's case, it's very apparent. Mexico's poverty rate is roughly 40 percent (i.e., 40 percent of the population live below the adjusted poverty line), while that of the United States is roughly 17 percent. Mexico's gross national income per capita is just $10,000. Most people there, especially rural people, are very poor by our standards. Mexico's rampant poverty presents a real problem both for Mexico and America, and I think we can all wish that the good people of Mexico were better off financially. As a human, I say that altruistically, but as an American, I say it selfishly: A poor Mexico puts undue economic pressure on America. The red white and blue has a bull's-eye on its back because of our wealth and prosperity.

After all, Mexicans who are simply looking for a better life elsewhere, or criminals who are looking to steal things of value to pad their wallets, can hardly look to exploit their southern neighbor, because Guatemala has one of the higher poverty rates in the world, barring some sub-Saharan African countries whose poverty levels hover around 60 percent. So, folks look for opportunities in wealthy America. We know this. So why am I stating the obvious?

As I've mentioned, one great way to cut into cartel crime is by strengthening Mexico's economy. I'm not implying the cartels would fold overnight, but through attrition over time, if more Mexican people were to make a better working wage, then fewer young men would be apt to join a cartel out of desperation. Fewer people, including government officials, would be so easily bribed. It's like the police here: When you are making a good wage at a job you value, taking a short-term bribe, which can cause you to lose it all if you are caught, is not a good business model.

But of course, the reality is we can't fix Mexico's economy by ourselves. At various times via various programs aimed at helping Mexican workers, we have tried. And we have failed. Until Mexico's leaders encourage these programs and welcome the help and transition to economic models that closely mirror ours, our attempts—as well as our huge financial investments—will be wasted.

There is a large faction in Mexico, including President Andrés Manuel López Obrador (AMLO) and at least a decent portion of the 54 percent of the population who elected him, that leans toward socialism. This book is not the time or the place to drill into the merits and shortcomings of economic systems but suffice it to say that socialism in Latin America has never resulted in a booming economy, but rather the kind of economic tragedy that leaves people starving and desperate enough to risk it all just to escape. Mexico is not there yet, but it *could* be if it doesn't make some changes soon. Just look at Venezuela.

In 2001, Venezuela was the richest country in South America, thanks largely to its oil reserves, which are thought to be second to none. But less than 15 years later, after a dictatorial leader Hugo Chavez had been elected under the promise of "wealth for all," and used the mandate to seize control of many private industries and resources there, its citizens were literally eating zoo animals to survive because they had already consumed their pets. But I digress.

Overhauling the Mexican economy to lift its people from poverty and to mitigate the temptation of crime *en masse* can't be done without serious political, social, and cultural changes to Mexico. Unfortunately, this change is out of the United States' immediate control, so we must look at other ways to hit the cartels to protect our own people.

A CULTURE OF CORRUPTION

Given our southern neighbor's inferior economy, one main reason why past efforts to curtail the cartels haven't worked, is, of course, Mexico's long-standing tradition of government corruption. Any college-age student who has ever attended spring break in Cancún, Cabo, Tijuana, or Matamoros knows about its corruption at a petty level. This petty-level corruption, from bribing a bouncer to give you favorable placement in line, paying a bartender to serve drinks to minors, or bribing a cop to look the other way while you illegally park, is baked into the culture. Unfortunately, it quickly morphs into major corruption if it becomes an accepted part of the culture.

While I don't agree with everything the United Nations is or does, it produced a succinct introductory paragraph written by Secretary-General Kofi Annan in its 2004 "Convention Against Corruption" paper. Annan wrote:

> *Corruption is an insidious plague that has a wide range of corrosive effects on societies. It undermines democracy and the rule of law, leads to violations of human rights, distorts markets, erodes the quality of life and allows organized crime, terrorism and other threats to human security to flourish.*[2]

By every metric, Mexico is plagued with corruption—corruption that has been embedded into the country's very DNA from the time it was formed. Spain, its Mexican colonies, and its business-class people were steeped in corruption, and in general they did not necessarily view the act of bribing as nefarious. It was just part of the culture. And we all know how hard cultural norms are to shake.

In modern Mexico, nepotism, doing favors for political points, and/or accepting money, gifts, and goods for business advantages are largely viewed as smart practice. At the very least, it's often written off as "just the way things are done." Of course, I believe anyone can discern a difference between giving a trusted friend or family member a cushy job, and accepting millions of dollars in exchange for illegal drugs entering a port under your watch. Sadly, the good people of Mexico live with corruption because that's the way it's always been, and because they can't do anything to change it. So, they must cope the best they can, under the system in which they live.

According to a survey given to average Mexicans in 2021, there are likely about 18,600 bribes accepted each day, or 7 million bribes paid per year in Mexico. A portion of these involve cartels bribing police or government officials. I could list hundreds of known instances where government officials were convicted of accepting bribes over the years, but we all know how to use Google.

One of the most recent and eye-popping cases, however, came to an end in mid-2023 when Mexico's own secretary of public security, Genaro Garcia Luna (the guy who was placed in charge of curtailing Mexico's cartel violence and the drug trade, i.e., the "architect of Mexico's war on drugs"), was convicted of taking millions in bribes from the cartels, even from El Chapo himself.

From 2006 to 2012, while he was serving in this high-ranking "drug czar" position of public trust—he was also president of the XXVIII International Drug Enforcement Conference (IDEC)—Luna would tip off cartels about planned raids, share intelligence with them, and, as head of the Mexico's anti-drug military forces, order the military to turn a blind eye at airports and other ports of entry so cartels could smuggle whatever they wanted in and out. And you better believe they did.

I could write another book about this guy and his crimes—hell, it would make a good movie—but the saddest part is, the only reason he was indicted and sentenced to 20 years in prison for cocaine trafficking among other charges is because he moved to the United States after his tenure so he could retire to the high life in Miami with his stores of laundered cash. By America's standards, Luna is as bad as bad actors come. But we may not be getting the full story of the pressure on this guy . . . not that I'm sticking up for him, because I'm certainly not. Let me explain:

In modern Mexico, where the cartels have so much wealth and access to officials, there is often more offered than just the carrot of increasing one's personal wealth that motivates some officials to work for the cartels. Some are served with an ultimatum: "We'll pay you handsomely if you help us, or . . . we will kill you and/or your family." I'm not justifying any form of accepting bribes, but the real threat of violent death is more real for Mexicans than it is for us.

For people in any area where law enforcement may already be corrupt, accepting the cartel's money *and* not getting murdered is a much better option than just getting murdered. I have no idea whether Luna was under threat of death, whether he was just greedy, or both. But it doesn't matter. U.S. federal agents nabbed Luna in Dallas in 2019.

This is but one anecdote of real corruption at Mexico's highest levels, corruption that directly affected America in the form of dangerous illegal drugs, including fentanyl, flooding our streets. It clearly illustrates the international criminal machine and government collusion that we are up against, because you have to figure that the officials who appointed him and to whom he reported, had to know about some of his corruption, and they were probably taking some kickbacks. In fact, in 2020, former U.S. Ambassador to Mexico Roberta S. Jacobson publicly asserted that the Calderón administration was aware of Luna's nefarious ties to the Sinaloa cartel. This was just three years ago. To think the Mexican government is now free of all cartel ties is naive as best.

On a local law enforcement level, corruption is even more rampant.

Consider that there are approximately 300,000 police officers in Mexico, or about 366 officers for every 100,000 people. The average police officer salary is just $350 per month—all for a very dangerous job. Most young men do not want to be police officers there. Keep in mind that an automobile is only slightly less expensive in Mexico than in the United States; therefore, it's difficult to see how many rank-and-file police officers could afford a new car. But although the job might be dangerous, and its base salary paltry, most who come into it know that the position may offer other, shall we say, more lucrative opportunities. And not all salary-padding bribes are from cartels. In fact, most of them aren't.

Of those 7 million bribes per year, most are taken in exchange for little things like tearing up parking tickets and petty crime. But again, no matter how small the bribe, when bribing becomes the standard, it's easy to see how large-scale bribing becomes the norm.

Of course, the Mexican government needs to clean this culture up by more harshly enforcing penalties for those caught giving and accepting bribes, but this is akin to asking Americans to quit betting on sports or to quit drinking.

Paying the officers a better wage in addition to enforcing penalties for accepting bribes might reduce some corruption, but this is impossible given the government's economic woes and impoverished people who can't afford to pay their water bill, much less be taxed on their minimal income. Quite simply, Mexico doesn't have the money to pay its law enforcement officers better, nor does it have the resources to hire more.

Certainly, not all criminals in Mexico buy their way out of crimes—not by a longshot. To prove this, all one need do is look at Mexico's untenable prison-overcrowding problem. And this is a good segue to Mexico's judicial system, which has historically differed from our own, not that ours is anywhere close to perfect.

MEXICO'S TRANSITIONING JUDICIAL INSTITUTIONS AND PATHETIC PRISONS

Another critical difference in the United States and Mexico, and one that needs to be solid and sound if Mexico is to make a dent in its cartel problem, is its judicial institutions.

Prior to 2008, Mexico operated under an "inquisitorial" system, where written evidence and documents were submitted to a judge, who then determined guilt or innocence. Trials were largely paperwork exercises without much open court debate. There are pros and cons to the inquisitorial system, but mostly cons if the country that employs such a system has a known problem with corruption and access to judges. Judges were, and still are, routinely threatened, killed, bribed, and extorted to give favorable rulings.

After 2008, Mexico began transitioning to an "adversarial" system, more like that in the United States. This system emphasizes oral trials with prosecuting and defense attorneys presenting their cases in open court. One advantage is that it tends to allow for greater transparency and due process of law.

While this more modern judicial style more closely resembles the U.S. system and sounds like a good idea, compared to the old system, there have been many problems with its implementation in Mexico, mainly stemming from the fact that it is new. People tend to be resistant to change, and lawyers and law professors haven't had generations of experience to train new lawyers in its nuances. Also, some Mexican people tend to be skeptical of a judicial system that can let people go on a procedural technicality, for example, especially when many of them are caused by inexperienced attorneys.

I'd love to report that this system is superior for Mexico, but until cartel influence is mitigated, and a new system has decades of use under its belt, Mexico's courts cannot be entirely trusted. As I mentioned earlier, judges there are routinely threatened and killed.

In June of 2020, the Jalisco Cartel murdered district court judge Uriel Villegas Ortiz and his wife, Verónica Barajas, in Colima, Mexico. It's tough to demand justice for your citizens if you can't even protect your judges.

In general, juveniles in Mexico are tried to be rehabilitated rather than imprisoned. This sounds good on its face, until you realize what I've already highlighted in previous chapters: Cartels employ kids as young as possible to do their bidding, because they know they will face lesser penalties. What's more, cartels have the money to buy the best lawyers; they know exactly how to use the system against itself.

But the most important part of all of this is that if someone, perhaps a known cartel member who has committed an atrocious crime, is convicted and sent to prison, there is little confidence that he won't be seen back in his cartel post in a matter of days.

That's because Mexico's prisons are ridiculously over capacity, corrupt to the core, and co-opted by the cartels, and the state has little money to do anything about it. If you think American prisons are corrupt and rife with drugs, crime, gangsters, and guards looking the other way, then you ain't seen nothin' yet.

The result is Mexican courts often send people to prison only as a last resort for the most heinous of crimes committed by nonconnected people. But in plenty of cases, it doesn't matter anyway, because a good portion of Mexico's prisons are fully controlled by the cartels.

How do you think El Chapo escaped the so-called maximum security *Puente Grande* prison in 2001? I'll give you a hint. The prison was nicknamed *Puerta Grande*, which means "Big Door."

The Jalisco Cartel controlled it. The Jalisco Cartel let El Chapo out. And the Mexican government knew the Jaliscos controlled it. They knew he'd escape.

In truth, Mexico's CERESO prison system (a Spanish acronym meaning "Center for Social Readaptation") is a joke, and everyone knows it. Guards are corrupted in the same ways as police—by threat, bribe, or both. By most accounts, Mexico's prisons are little more than breeding grounds for cartel recruits—gangster hotels—places where cartels can kill and extort inmates and rival gang members as they wish; sell drugs, contract prostitutes and personal chefs to cook them dinner, they come and go as they please to make hits and deals; operate as if the prison were a criminal headquarters where the lights are (sometimes) kept on by the state. Even if a court bravely sentences a cartel member to prison, the member tries to hide his smile like Brer Rabbit as he is ushered out in ceremonial handcuffs, where photos are taken so the government can show the world its valiant crime-ridding efforts.

If Mexico has any hope of controlling the cartels, a priority must be to completely overhaul its prison system to get it ready for all of the violent criminals it will soon be receiving. But that will take time, resolve, bloodshed, and an amount of money that the Mexican government doesn't have.

As it stands now, Mexico's penal system is likely contributing more to the crime, drug, and cartel problem than fixing it.

POLICE OR MILITARY?

Mexico's national military comprises a ground-based army (Ejército Mexicano), a sea-based navy (Secretaría de Marina or SEMAR), various special forces units, and, most recently, a national guard-type organization consisting of part-time soldiers that was designed to mimic ours.

In the last 30 years, Mexico's army has been employed when cartel violence has reached fever-pitch, but experience has proven that even this army, whose units are well versed in the guerrilla-style warfare that has plagued Central and South America for decades, is not flexible enough to face civilian-type enemies who strategically use civilian-packed cities and streets to their advantage. Special forces units, many of whom were trained off the record by the CIA and other western counter-insurgency consultants, have proven ineffective as well, largely due to the lack of will and/or the corruption of those who have employed them. National guard units—a hybrid-style police force composed of locals with military-style training—would seem to offer a solution, but even that has failed to intimidate, much less destroy, the cartels.

While the Mexican government, under various regimes, has at times marched out some of its federal forces—sometimes more for show and, in a few cases, for real—historically, Mexico has tried to solve its cartel and drug problem via local law enforcement, just as we do. The difference is, after our mafia was largely destroyed, there is no criminal force in America with anywhere near the power, reach, or influence as the cartels have in Mexico.

I'll admit it again. As a former Homeland Security official, I previously thought using properly trained law enforcement resources—i.e., local police—was a sound strategy. That opinion was formed only after witnessing some of the disasters that using a traditional military in a local law-enforcement capacity often causes. For an overused analogy, it's like using an axe when a scalpel is needed. Mexico's military units of even 20 years ago were not properly equipped or trained to handle domestic problems wherein the enemy is loose in its organization, supremely mobile, dynamic in its mission, and intertwined among everyday people. And they are still not ready.

Local law enforcement, at least in America, deals with specific people in specific communities each day; experienced officers know the lay of the land and the intimate intel that can best be gleaned by living there. However, the same personalized advantage that rank-and-file officers have in policing a community is also a weakness; on their own, they are easy to corrupt. Cartels also know exactly who they are and where they live. It's got to suck being a cop in Mexico.

As we've learned over the last two decades, however, also inept are Mexico's paramilitary Narco forces, which have been mobilized from time to time when cartel leaders have challenged government leaders or when public outcry has reached such a crescendo that it has threatened the outcomes of elections.

Pablo Escobar was perhaps the most obvious and ruthless example when, in the 1980s, he waged outright war on the Colombian government by blowing up cars and buildings and assassinating government officials, judges, journalists, and nearly 500 police officers, often in broad daylight. Not only did it scare the wits out of public officials, but the violence wasn't well received by the public either. When the cartels reach such a large size, fighting them can look more like civil war than merely a few SWAT teams making swift arrests of local villains.

Since Escobar established the model, there have been many more overt acts of terrorism upon governmental authority by the cartels.

In 2006, then-Mexican president Felipe Calderón initiated what, on its face, appeared to be an aggressive anti-cartel campaign. He sent around 50,000 soldiers as well as federal police to battle the cartels. While many cartel leaders were either arrested or killed, he didn't finish the job. Perhaps he had struck a deal with one or more of the cartels to rid it of its competition, or perhaps the public grew weary of the war zones created in their streets. Either way, the result was that Calderón, ever the spineless politician, backed off before the job was finished.

Indeed, in about every case, the Mexican government has backed down rather than persistently hounded the killers to their lairs. And when the government's will wanes, Mexican military members, including their leaders, often become corrupted as well. We witnessed it in Afghanistan, among other regions, as we battled a localized enemy—ISIS—whose members were often intertwined with the community. Good people are reluctant to reveal themselves by turning on a domestic enemy if they think they will be abandoned and left to fend for themselves. This has happened time and time again in Mexico, and it's usually the minimally paid soldiers and policemen who get screwed. Many police, soldiers, and even citizens are reluctant to make the same mistake twice. Indeed, many Mexican citizens believe that the cartels will be around longer than any administration, and so they think it's a better bet to team up with better-paying cartels than with a government that's often seen as corrupt itself.

There's a reason why plenty of cartel members you see in recent photos look more like soldiers of a state-run military unit, even holding fully automatic military weapons and grenades attached to their bulletproof vests: It's because they were trained by branches of the military, and then defected to the cartels, where they retained their weapons and training that they now use against their enemies. Why? The cartels offer these soldiers more than their own government does in terms of pay, protection, and prestige.

One example is when, in 1999, commandos from one of Mexico's elite military units defected to the Gulf Cartel that promised them riches in exchange for carrying out its security duties as well as its hits. In 2010, this heavily armed faction that was intimidated by no one broke away from the Gulf Cartel, forming the Zeta Cartel. It's one reason why the Zetas, even today, are so well trained, well equipped, and downright scary. It is essentially a paramilitary organization that sells illegal goods and uses extortion as its business model. It is ruthless in nature.

As I've illustrated, neither Mexico's military units nor its local police/law enforcement agencies have been effective against the cartels in any meaningful way. But if you're an honest Mexican president who is determined to battle them at all costs, and you must pick a gladiator, it's got to be the military, or more specifically, hand-picked, specialized military units As I mentioned, my view on this dilemma has evolved over the last few years, mainly because the cartels and their power have evolved; the cartels are not just a domestic problem anymore, but an international one that affects our own security!

As it stands now, local Mexican police simply do not have the training, the weapons, the intelligence resources, the resistance to corruption, or the sheer numbers in terms of manpower to fight the cartels. While it is possible that if the Mexican citizens had Second Amendment–type rights and were armed as well as our citizens are, they could stand up to cartels on a local, long-term basis, making it very difficult for the cartels to operate unconcernedly in the light of day. Certainly, it would take years of steadfast resolve, and it would be bloody. But it's hardly worth mentioning because its people aren't well armed, and I'm not even sure the Mexican culture would support it. If you've carved out a life in the face of cartel control, you likely aren't too motivated to risk it.

Therefore, the Mexican military—all branches—is the only force in Mexico that has the potential and the political access to do so. And I believe it could, if its leadership had the guts and the integrity to truly employ it and all of its resources—including trusted local police—to defeat them.

There is, however, another force that could track the cartels to their fentanyl labs, stash houses, and lavish haciendas if they had the authority to do so. That is, America's Special Forces. Unfortunately, like Mexico's leaders, our current leadership lacks the will to force an ultimatum, or much more diplomatically, insist that Mexico let us help solve our mutual problem.

To be clear, I'm not blaming all the cartels' successes and Mexico's failures on inept or corrupted soldiers and policemen. Many of these people *are* risking it all to stand up for what they know is right—all for little personal reward. America, perhaps better than anyone except possibly Russia, knows that rooting out nondescript, well-funded combatants from local enclaves is a very, very difficult task. Rather, what I am saying is that clearly, for myriad reasons, the cartels are winning. And now they are threatening the national security of not only Mexico but also the United States.

ANTI-AMERICAN MOTIVES?

When we list reasons for Mexico's failings against the cartels and study some of the actions of its leaders, we must also consider the possibility that at least some of Mexico's leadership might secretly be OK with the added pressure placed on America by weak law enforcement and border security. After all, if non-tax-paying members of Mexico's lower class wish to flee across the border, thereby alleviating some of the strain on its resources while adding to America's burden, Mexico's leaders might correctly assume that, over time, this exchange could bolster their economy while weakening ours, thereby giving them more leverage for political and trade negotiations later.

We know China is doing it. They are not sending fentanyl, communicable viruses, TikTok, and disinformation campaigns to us as Christmas gifts; they are doing it to subtly weaken America over time. I'd hope Mexico is not doing the same, but sometimes I wonder. Still, it would be unwise to not consider this possibility as one reason for Mexico's lack of action against what most people on both sides of the border view as a common enemy.

What I do know is that Mexico's intentions can be discerned by bold, poignant—and ultimately symbiotic—foreign policy. If Mexico will not sort the problem out on its own and will not let us assist, then we can assume the worst in its intentions. After all, why wouldn't Mexico want its cartel problem to end?

As the state of the union stands now, however, the Biden administration is failing to secure America by diplomacy, by leverage, by bargaining, by enforcement, or by force. Despite Mayorkas' gaslighting quote of "We have a plan, and that plan is working," neither Congress nor the American public have seen a comprehensive border and immigration strategy plan from this administration.

Rather, it's allowing Mexico to sit back and watch as its problems intensify and become ours. The trouble is, in years past, these problems were centered on illegal drugs. Now they have mushroomed into a full-fledged national security threat.

We cannot afford to simply stand by and hope that good will win out on its own.

AMERICA THE SCAPEGOAT

Perhaps the most maddening thing for Americans today is that, in addition to feeling the effects of Mexico's failures, they know they are also being lied to by their own government on the issue. If our own government says anything official about the borders or the burgeoning drug trade, it typically blames America—specifically Trump's policies—for the problems Mexico continues to export over the border.

For example, if Americans get killed while vacationing in Mexico, they say Americans should have known better than to travel there. If kids get trafficked across the border as sex slaves, it's America's fault for creating a market for perverts. If citizens die of drug overdoses, it's due to our country's hopelessly unfair culture that creates insatiable addictions. If terrorists sneak across the border hoping to bomb us, it's due to what we did in Guantanamo Bay and in Iraq.

Look, I'm not saying America doesn't have problems. There is no denying that our collective drug demand is off the charts, and it must be addressed; it's embarrassing to admit that both the legal and illegal drug markets here should not be as big as they are. There should be no market at all for the abominable sin of child exploitation and slavery. It's inexcusable, and we should take responsibility by making sure that none of the animals who commit these acts ever get out of jail when they are caught. Furthermore, as opportunistic capitalists, too many of us take advantage of cheap labor when we could be hurting our domestic labor force by doing so. The point is, we have much work to do. America has always held itself accountable, and it will continue to do so.

It's also about time that we start calling out Mexico for its shortcomings and failures. As previously stated, Mexico itself is a giant market for drugs. (Did you know that due to America's lax marijuana laws, it's thought that more pot is now moving *from* San Diego into Tijuana than the other way?)

I believe our drug addicts would not have access to as many illicit drugs if Mexico weren't supplying them. We wouldn't be losing 60,000 to 70,000 per year to fentanyl, that's for certain. Our resources and our citizens wouldn't be as taxed if Mexico were to put a little effort into convincing its people not to flee across the border *en masse*. Perhaps it could get a handle on its own corruption and crime that spills over onto its charitable neighbor, whom it readily asks for handouts with the guiltless frequency of a four-year-old.

We love the Mexican people and their rich culture, and we give them millions of dollars each year in foreign aid. We fund much of their tourism industry, and we keep them safe from foreign threats by way of our stature and kindness alone. A better Mexico equals a better America, no doubt. But it's high time that Mexico gives a little love back or, at the very least, helps us help them.

How do we get Mexico to do that? By way of better policy and a strategic plan to tackle the cartels. I'll explain in the next chapters.

CHAPTER NINE

Combating the Cartels: The Marino Approach

These drug cartels represent a clear and present danger to the national security of the United States.

—Fictional U.S. President Donald Moffat in
the 1994 movie *Clear and Present Danger*

I f you've read this far, you're intimately aware of the problems that have combined to undermine America's national security. But please humor me as I summarize the situations as succinctly as possible before I introduce a plan for solving what I believe to be America's greatest current threat: Mexico's cartels—terrorists—working to facilitate the entrance of jihadi terrorists into our homeland.

As you know, we have an unsecure border combined with an unconstitutional immigration policy that allows thousands of illegal immigrants into the country daily. (On September 29, 2023, just as I started writing this chapter, the Border Patrol reported that it had made contact with over 10,000 immigrants who had been trying to cross illegally or triple the average daily amount of just a few months prior.) Meanwhile, Mexico is home to multiple well-funded, well-armed, and extremely dangerous cartels that are exploiting our porous borders and favorable policies to traffic drugs, fentanyl, human slaves, ISIS-style terrorists, and violence into our homeland at will; this illicit business results in thousands of dead Americans day after day. Mexico has failed in its past attempts at dismantling the cartels, and neither it nor our own government seems to be interested in solving the problem. I do not say this lightly, as I realize it's a serious charge. But by looking objectively at the administration's actions that repeatedly place a higher priority on the welfare of immigrants rather than its own citizens, it's difficult to view it any other way. In the nicest of terms, enemies of the United States are exploiting our compassion.

It seems like the deck is stacked against the American people. So, what, if anything, can be done to dam the river of terrorists before it's too late?

My approach is a multiphase, six-step list of imperative actions. Of course, there will be more steps as policies, politics, and countermeasures as terrorists evolve, but without these initial actions, positive change will become increasingly more difficult as time goes by.

The good news is that it's not as complex as some people would have you believe, especially if you have America's interests as the primary goal. Certainly, my plan is bold compared to the politically correct plans of weak-kneed politicians. No doubt, it will ruffle the feathers of some globalists who see any hardline approach as a xenophobic assault on humanity itself.

But if progressives are going to fight for all the causes that they think are important into the future—LGBTQ rights, abortion rights, climate change initiatives, and so on—they must come to understand that America must have its sovereignty if those causes are to be championed via our democratic process. The enemies at our gates and in our homeland despise democracy, just as they generally despise Western progressive causes.

So, how do we ensure our sovereignty and ability to make laws that most people in various constituencies approve? We do it by unemotionally protecting our homeland from unmitigated foreign invasion at all costs. So, I believe all Americans, not just the conservative Right, should get behind my plan. As I've echoed many times, however, we cannot install comprehensive immigration reform—something nearly everyone wants, albeit for differing reasons—until we have secure borders. Here's how we can do it.

Elect pro-American leaders who place national security as their highest priority. I'd like to think there is a way to convince the Biden administration that its border policies are, in fact, crushing America so that it might reverse course, but evidence suggests this will not happen. It is too radical in its progressive agendas, it is too beholden to special interest groups, and it is still convinced that doing the opposite of what Trump did *must* be the right path forward. A portion of the public has tried to shame the administration by demonstrating that its border policies encourage migrants to risk their lives coming here, all while emboldening terrorists . . . but the evidence is continually ignored. So, I'm convinced that the only way to usher in more effective policy is to usher in a new "Americans Before Aliens" administration and Congress.

This step is the most important, but also the toughest to accomplish due to the political polarity that has besieged us. Still, it must happen. We must elect leaders who understand that abiding by the tenets of the Constitution—especially law and order—is vital to our republic. Some of those tenets are securing America's borders; installing a regulated system of reasonable immigration that vets immigrants primarily based on their merits and swiftly deports criminal aliens; and using any means necessary to combat the cartels to stem the flow of human trafficking, pandemic-level drugs, violent gang members, and terrorists. A new administration also must strive for more robust law enforcement by increasing funding for state and local police, and by appointing a pro-law-and-order Department of Justice, nonactivist federal prosecutors, and federal judges who will incarcerate homegrown criminals as soon as they are convicted, and criminal aliens as soon as they are caught.

Without the help of the president, the secretary of Homeland Security, Congress, and other key leaders, we cannot employ the following steps that are necessary to ensure our nation's security. These leaders set policy, make laws, decide whom and how to prosecute, and influence the actions of other countries. While most Democrats care more about protecting Americans than foreigners, the Biden administration isn't among them. If it were, it wouldn't destroy the border wall and weld border gates permanently open; it wouldn't sue Texas Governor Greg Abbott for installing river barriers in the Rio Grande; it wouldn't allow millions of unvetted illegal immigrants to skip the established immigration system to flood into the country and take from programs that would otherwise help our poor; it wouldn't give taxpayer money to NGOs to serve illegal aliens in our already-stressed cities; it wouldn't drop the vaccine/immunization requirements for illegal immigrant children who enroll in our taxpayer-funded schools, thereby endangering our kids; and it wouldn't threaten to sue any state or American entity who objects to any of this anti-American, Constitution-defying policy.

As crazy as all its actions are to the American people, this administration is not insane. It may be complicit and/or incompetent, but it's not insane. It knows exactly what it's doing as it unravels our layered systems of security and undermines our culture. And so, it's our duty as Americans to vote Biden and Harris out of office and elect leaders—Democrat, Republican, or Independent—who will put Americans first.

Appropriate funding from Congress that will pay for a thorough plan that will be focused on protecting Americans. The most obvious mechanism to accomplish this is by passing H.R. 2, the "Secure the Border Act of 2023."

Consider this: As of July 2023, U.S. taxpayers have spent between $76 and $115 billion (it's unconscionable that we don't know the exact amount) on defending *Ukraine's* borders. Rest assured, we will be spending much more in the months and years to come. (No doubt, we will be spending an unfathomable amount on Israel's security, too, after the despicable events of October 7, 2023, carried out by Hamas.) You may agree or disagree with the purpose of this spending, but the point is this: What we have spent on defending the sovereignty of another nation in just three years is more than the annual gross national product of 114 countries! It's a lot of money, any way you slice it. Even a fraction of this amount would do wonders for our own border and our national security. Hell, it might solve those problems.

Trump's wall, for example, will cost around 12 billion. Intelligence, technology (including drones, cameras, apps, biometric capturing systems, license plate readers, lidar systems to detect underground tunnels, and more), man hours, and fully funded law enforcement operations would be a drop in the bucket compared to what we are spending to defend a non-NATO country half a world away.

Of course, any such comprehensive security action on a grand scale requires grand funding, to be sure, and the only way it can be appropriated to America's border crisis is via Congress. And what is the best way to instigate congressional action? Its constituents must demand it. So, we need grassroots campaigns—concerned citizens mobilizing, peacefully protesting, writing letters to their congressmen, and generally keeping this issue front and center—to ensure that it happens. Only after money is appropriated and specifically earmarked for combating the cartels and closing the border via a tactical plan can we begin to make a dent in such an entrenched foe.

Officially change the designation of the cartels from transnational criminal organizations (TCOs) to foreign terrorist organizations (FTOs) so we can take the fight to the cartels, using any means necessary, including the U.S. military and its intelligence networks.

Doing so gives us much more legal leeway and leverage in dealing with these nimble, well-funded, covert, and loosely structured organizations that must be fought on multiple fronts, in various jurisdictions in myriad ways, often using nonconventional tactics.

Official U.S. State Department's language defines FTOs as:

. . . foreign organizations that are designated by the Secretary
of State in accordance with Section 219 of the Immigration
and Nationality Act (INA), as amended. FTO designations
play a critical role in our fight against terrorism and are an
effective means of curtailing support for terrorist activities
and pressuring groups to get out of the terrorism business.

Furthermore, state department language reminds us that a sitting U.S. president can designate FTOs by fiat:

Executive Order 13224 gives the U.S. Government a
powerful tool to impede terrorist funding and is part of our
national commitment to lead the international effort to bring
a halt to the evil of terrorist activity. In general terms, the
Order provides a means by which to disrupt the financial
support network for terrorists and terrorist organizations by
authorizing the U.S. government to designate and block the
assets of foreign individuals and entities that commit, or pose
a significant risk of committing, acts of terrorism.

Where it gets more complicated, however, stems from the fact that the cartels are private entities that exist in the sovereign nation of Mexico. As for this, you might recall back in 2001 with the passage of the Patriot Act that gave way to the following legal code on state sponsors of terrorism:

Countries determined by the Secretary of State to have
repeatedly provided support for acts of international terrorism
are designated pursuant to three laws: section 6(j) of the
Export Administration Act, Section 40 of the Arms Export

Control Act, and section 620A of the Foreign Assistance Act.
Taken together, the four main categories of sanctions resulting
from designation under these authorities include restrictions
on U.S. foreign assistance; a ban on defense exports and
sales; certain controls over exports of dual use items; and
miscellaneous financial and other restrictions. Designation
under the above-referenced authorities also implicates other
sanctions laws that penalize persons and countries engaging in
certain trade with state sponsors.

In late August of 2023, during the Republican presidential debates, candidate Vivek Ramaswamy suggested (as former President Trump had done in the past) that the U.S. military could take unilateral action against the cartels within Mexico. A few days later, Representative Dan Crenshaw, a Republican from Texas, tweeted a message to Mexican President López Obrador, asking him why he opposes a proposal the congressman had introduced in January 2023 that would have authorized military force in Mexico to combat the cartels. After all, to most people who believe the cartels are a common problem and enemies of both America and Mexico, López Obrador's reply might come as a baffling, if not an antagonistic, surprise:

"In addition to being irresponsible, it is an offense to the people of Mexico," he said. "Mexico does not take orders from anyone."

That rings more than a little ironic to me, knowing that many of Mexico's officials have been proven to take orders from the cartels. It also makes me question whose team López Obrador is on.

If you didn't view his words as being antagonistic toward the United States, consider that a few days later, Tijuana Mayor

Montserrat Caballero and the prior Mexican foreign secretary Marcelo Ebrard implanted a piece of the Berlin Wall near the United States–Mexico border in Tijuana with the following inscription:

May this be a lesson to build a society that knocks down walls and builds bridges.

I think "bridge building," in a diplomatic sense, means helping each other solve mutual problems—not building a literal bridge into one country so that the others can dump its problems on the other while sapping its resources. So, thanks for that, Mayor Caballero. You are so helpful!

The point is, if within Mexico's borders live entities that are clear and present threats to Mexico's national security as well as ours, yet that country's government fails to make any real attempt to defeat it, or even allow us to help them defeat it, when can Mexico officially be deemed by our government to be harboring—in a functional sense, aiding and abetting—terrorists?

To be clear, I believe that at this point, Mexico is a state sponsor of terrorism. At the very least, the U.S. government—namely currently serving Secretary of State Antony Blinken—should issue Mexico's government an ultimatum to prove otherwise. We've got to know whether Mexico is with us or against us. We've learned that middle ground doesn't work, for it gives the terrorists too many convenient places to hide.

Believe me, I don't like war, and I don't like sending our troops any more places than we absolutely must send them to defend the country. But if Mexico cannot or will not battle the imminent threat that its FTOs present, then *we* must. The good news is that when you are the United States, whom Mexico dearly depends on, there are many ways of persuasion that do not involve actual military action . . . which leads to my next step.

Place pressure on Mexico to help us defeat the cartels. How do we do this? For starters, consider that Mexico receives millions of dollars in foreign aid from us. It should not see another dime until it agrees to let us help. Again, I'm merely asking Mexico to let us help tackle the cartels, and not demanding that it tackle its problems alone, as many countries with our power would likely do. What's not to like about this proposal if you're from Mexico and not a cartel member?

Similarly, we should stop all foreign aid going to South American illegal immigrant producers such as Venezuela and El Salvador. There are simply too many cases of fraud when one government gives to another corrupt government with a hand-shake and the hollow words "Make sure this goes to the people who need it most, will ya?" Enough of that racket until these countries start helping us in a meaningful way.

Mexico and other countries in the natural line of northerly migration should be compelled to take on claims of asylum from those who enter their own borders from other countries. (The Trump administration tried to pass a law mandating that immigrants seeking asylum who pass through other countries on their way to the United States must apply for asylum in one of those countries first. But it was shot down in federal court in June of 2020.) A person coming from Venezuela, for example, should not get a free pass and a high-five of *"Buena suerte!"* ("Good luck!") as they traverse Colombia, Panama, and all the other countries in line before they reach America. These countries must protect their borders and follow their laws on immigration, as well. And if they don't, they should expect their monthly paychecks from generous ol' Uncle Sam to dwindle.

Finally, Mexico must reform its prisons by using its military to regain control of them, and it must impose strict penalties on drug traffickers, human traffickers, fentanyl chemists, and anyone who illegally tries to cross its borders in any direction with illicit items.

We can do this the hard way, without Mexico, or the easier way *with* it. We must give Mexico's people the incentive to help us while letting them know that we are in the battle with them for the long haul. We must persistently send messages to its citizens that it's in both countries' best interest to destroy the FTOs that master them. We must give Mexico's leaders a hardline ultimatum. *Join us now in this battle, or we'll do it ourselves.* But if we do it ourselves, we won't be responsible for any collateral damage to its leaders' castles, bank accounts, privileged positions, or futures in office.

Once an agreement is reached that allows our intelligence efforts and possibly our Special Forces operators into Mexico and its airspace, we must be open to using every high-tech tool and trained specialist in our arsenal to find FTOs, surveil them, gain intel on their crimes and lifestyles, and then use precision strikes or raids to arrest and/or kill them. If we arrest them, they must be swiftly extradited to America until Mexico's prison systems are overhauled. I'm not expecting that anytime soon.

With over 20 years' experience in doing these very things in terribly prohibitive places, such as Afghanistan and Pakistan, I guarantee our Special Forces, if given rein to do what they do best, can conduct these types of targeted, intel-heavy counterinsurgency operations with frighteningly positive results in Mexico. We have scores of war-hardened dudes with thermal goggles, drones, silenced M4s, stealth helicopters, and plenty of motivation who are begging for the opportunity to do it. I believe Mexico's citizens, bless their hearts, can be persuaded to give us intel much more readily than Pakistanis can, mainly because we have so much in common, including religion. But most shouldn't need much persuasion. At the time of this writing, nine Mexican cities rank in many top 10 lists of the world's most dangerous. This should be nothing less than appalling to anyone in America or Mexico, and incentive enough for helping us help them.

Of course, we'd also need to coordinate efforts with the CBP, ICE, and even the National Guard where large-scale, incorruptible security is needed. We'd bolster border security to prevent more cartel members from fleeing as their homelands and hideouts heat up. The fact is, America has too many troops stationed needlessly all over the world to be absent on our own home front. Many of these patriots would be best utilized where their country now needs them most: shoulder to shoulder, Humvee to Humvee, field of fire to field of fire, dotted along in unison with a clear goal, on our southern border.

Simultaneously, we'd use our existing law enforcement, DEA, and intelligence task forces domestically to conduct raids on known cartel members, terrorists, and fentanyl labs operating within the United States. We'd incarcerate those who are found guilty to the maximum extent of the law. We'd pressure known affiliates—street gangs—to turn on them, just as we did with the mafia back in the 1980s.

In essence, we'd take the fight to the FTOs.

I don't say this lightly, because I don't like spilling American blood. I'm not a warmonger, but I truly believe that if we don't do it now, more innocent American lives will be unnecessarily taken in the future. If our leaders are bold in their language to Mexico, however, our own military action will not be necessary.

Demand that our state and federal lawmakers increase the penalties for manufacturing, trafficking, selling, buying, or receiving fentanyl and its spinoffs.

I'm the first one to admit that the war on drugs has been abysmal, if not a complete failure. As we've learned the hard way, banning things that many Americans want is traditionally not a good solution—especially if those items can be readily made. Border walls do little. I'm even open to having a serious conversation about legalizing some drugs that could arguably have a negative effect on cartel money and a positive effect on drug-trade violence in our cities. It might also help get less-dangerous and more-taxable products to those who choose to use drugs. Again, history shows that mass drug and alcohol bans haven't worked, so we need to explore options to better regulate the U.S. drug market, since we cannot destroy it.

On the other hand, we *can* reasonably control some things that cannot be readily made. Just consider nuclear weapons, complex large-scale poisons, or the COVID-19 pandemic. Historically in America, when a drug or disease comes along that is as dangerous as fentanyl, Earth-moving steps—the full combined force of America's power—are taken to mitigate its proliferation. Fentanyl is so dangerous that it *is* essentially a poison and not a drug. According to the DEA, just two kilos of it—an amount that's easily stashed in a small backpack—can kill one million people. This is a substance that on the danger scale is more like ricin, anthrax, or cyanide than most recreational drugs, and so it should be classified as such. Those who deal it—and especially those who make it (mostly Chinese chemists), along with the cartels who traffic it for profit—know this. Hell, even most drug users don't want their recreational drugs laced with fentanyl either, because most of them are looking for a good time—not death!

Anyone caught dealing fentanyl should be prosecuted for attempted murder. Test strips are readily available, so I don't want to hear the "I didn't know my product was laced!" defense when 10 teenagers at a party die from the fentanyl-laced drugs sold to them hours earlier. Penalties should be harsh, because the stakes are so high. If a person accidentally takes, or even accidentally handles, fentanyl, they can die. As I mentioned earlier, toddlers are dying at a heartbreaking rate from this stuff. It's a direct threat to the lives of police officers daily.

I hate to use the overused term "zero-tolerance," but legally we should have zero tolerance for anyone who makes, traffics, or deals fentanyl—especially if they are illegal aliens. By "especially," I mean that criminal aliens don't have all the rights afforded to U.S. citizens. So, they should be prosecuted swiftly, harshly, and by using as little of our court resources as possible. Death sentences for trafficking that results in death should not be off the table.

For anyone who believes that punishment isn't a deterrent for drug dealers; let's try it for a couple years and see for ourselves after we have more data. If, after examining the data, we find that it doesn't work, we'll admit it and try something else. I've got lots of ideas.

Stop all federal public safety grants going to sanctuary cities and counties until they provide detailed plans that will prioritize the enforcement of federal immigration law and criminal prosecution, and cease to protect illegal aliens unlawfully.

The jurisdictions that have abandoned law and order to promote their progressive political agendas serve as a pull factor for illegal immigration. In essence, they encourage it by placing a welcome mat out—a literal red carpet at hotel entrances in many cases—for illegal immigration. Once there, illegal immigrants can't be deported nearly as easily as they should be if they are found to be in violation of our laws. As proven in many recent criminal busts, criminal aliens who are looking to hide from law enforcement use these cities as vast enclaves in which to blend in and hide. Sanctuary policies must be eliminated.

As I was writing this, a Brazilian national and criminal alien named Danelo Cavalcante, who was wanted for murder in Brazil and the brutal stabbing murder of his American girlfriend, escaped federal prison in Philadelphia and was on the run. Although he was eventually apprehended, I want to know: How did he get here in the first place? I have no idea, and if our immigration authorities know, they aren't admitting it. What *is* clear is that this carnivorous animal wasn't stopped by our Border Patrol or our policies. It appears he wasn't vetted at all. And he took the life of an American. There are thousands of similar stories wherein criminal aliens have raped, murdered, and robbed Americans. Why should we give these lawless, society-wrecking savages any type of sanctuary?

Sanctuary cities defy federal law and therefore those laws must be eradicated. Either we are a country of law and order, or we are not. We can't be both. And as a democratic republic, if we choose to be a sanctuary nation, we must be prepared for the results. We will soon not be the kind, charitable country that we know to be the envy of the world. Sanctuary policies will quickly turn us into the same types of places from which thousands of good people flee daily.

CHAPTER TEN

Turning the Political Tide at Home

Majority of Americans say there is an "invasion" at the southern border.

—NPR.Org headline, August, 18, 2022

Right now in America, there is a political divide that runs much deeper than a debate about gender affirmation, guns, or abortion. Judging from polls that would shock both Democrats and Republicans of even the 1990s, its apparent that a frightening amount of people wish to demolish the very pillars of society on which America was founded, including its capitalistic economic system, its freedom of speech, its law and order, its basis in Christianity, and its reliance on private individuals to forge their own path through life by free will and determination. Most of us can agree that America was built by immigrants. Most of us welcome more eager immigrants who respect our established laws and work to make America better. Around 50 percent of American citizens say they want an immigration system that welcomes more people.

Yet, a much smaller subgroup of this set claims to want open borders. This same group, the radical progressive Left, tends to categorize those who do not want open borders as racists or white supremacists who yearn for a return of the "good ol' days" of Jim Crow and other despicable and abolished policies of America's past. The other side rejects this ridiculous notion and instead argues that the progressives despise the core values on which America was founded.

The result is an age of ideological warfare, with America's future hanging in the balance. As of 2023, the radical Left appears to be winning. But the tide may be starting to turn.

You see, through all of this there is at least one issue that I believe both of the more moderate sides can reasonably agree on, and that is this: If Americans and American citizens-to-be had their choice, none would want cartel members, human traffickers, terrorists, or any other persons who would do them harm taking the space in America that could go to good-natured, lawful immigrants who simply want a better life here. Surely, we can agree on this.

If we can, then there is only one way to attempt to accomplish this vision without broadly classifying entire groups of people by religion, wealth, proximity, nationality, skin color, or other traits to determine their immigration value. The method is by thorough vetting of each immigrant who wishes to enter, *before* they enter. It's not easy, cheap, or fast. But it's the only way.

If we can all agree that there should be vetting involved in the immigration process to attempt to screen out bad actors, then there is only one logical way to accomplish it: by first securing our borders.

We must filter all hopeful immigrants through official points of entry where they can best be vetted by obtaining relevant biological information, background information, and necessary paperwork to document their existence.

Concurrently, we must have robust enforcement of our immigration laws to ensure that people don't purposefully avoid the vetting system altogether. In this way, if anyone tries to bypass a port of entry to sneak into the country unlawfully, it can be assumed that this person is nefarious—criminal by definition—since he or she tried to enter by breaking our laws. If this person is caught, there must be stiff penalties imposed, including losing the right to attempt to enter America lawfully in the future. Title 8. This is only fair to Americans, and only fair to lawful immigrants who invest great personal time, money, and resources in navigating America's immigration system in the legal way.

This might sound like a hardline stance to some people who seem to be more offended by wrong pronouns than by murder, but, trust me, it's the standard border and immigration policy for most of the world. Indeed, to most people in the history of the world, the simple steps I've summarized are common sense.

We simply cannot regulate immigration or vet those coming in if they arrive without documentation, illegally, via cracks in the fence or an app that depends on the honor system. The Biden administration's crown jewel, its updated (and dumbed-down) CBP One app, which was simply designed to let unvetted immigrants in easily while figuring out what to do with them later, is not the answer either. Too many of these unvetted people are providing false information and disappearing into our country. Surely, most are good people at heart. Surely, many are not.

The American people must demand that their government, via whatever party is in charge, take every step possible to secure the border. (After all, DHS is called the Department of Homeland Security—not the Department of Easy Immigration.) Not doing so will maintain or exacerbate many problems, which most of us on the right or the left do not desire. These include:

- Increased transnational terrorist organization (cartel) business, power, and influence
- More inhumane treatment of immigrants: On September 12, 2023, the International Organization for Migration announced that the "U.S. Mexico border is the world's deadliest migration land route" with "686 deaths and disappearances . . . of migrants in 2022."
- More human trafficking victims
- More fentanyl, drug crime and more accidental deaths
- More acts of terrorism and more 9/11-style tragedies
- Overcrowded cities and overburdened resources, including our welfare, transit, and education systems
- Bordertown-style violence in cities and eventually in small towns

We must have political consensus by the public to mandate border security from its representatives in Congress. We can decide on the numbers of immigrants, vetting systems, welfare budgets for transitioning migrants, and other immigration details like DACA later. But we cannot do this when ten thousand people are coming into the country, mostly undocumented, daily. As a sovereign nation, if we continue to allow unfettered, at-will immigration to happen, eventually we will be sovereign no more.

Don't get me wrong, I love Latin American food and culture, but I am not too keen on the thought of its cartel operators giving us orders, killing our leaders and journalists, corrupting our children, and generally extorting our country via threats of violence. I'm also not so enthusiastic about waking up to another 9/11, courtesy of the terrorists we let in because we didn't want to insult their dignity while they were being vetted for entry.

Americans must know that if we continue the same Wild West, lawless immigration path that we are currently on, there will be fighting in the streets of the United States. Likely, the government won't call it a "war," because that would be bad optically and economically in the eyes of our trading partners, but rest assured, that is exactly what it will be as desperate Americans are faced with no other choice than to forcefully take back their communities from criminal elements who aren't held accountable by our hijacked justice departments and defunded police. If we are to avoid warfare, we must challenge some of our own local politicians who implement policies that encourage illegal immigration and crime. Here are a few of the first steps I propose.

First, we must strengthen, not weaken, our law enforcement agencies across the nation. When progressive leaders cut their law enforcement budgets for political points, it's the poor and the downtrodden who suffer most—especially when the affluent people leave. What these leaders should have done was increase their budgets for higher-quality law officer recruitment and training. Higher-caliber, better-trained officers mean fewer police officer mistakes. When leaders support their police while also holding them to a higher standard of accountability, both police morale and public trust in the police can begin to be restored.

If local leaders do not support their police departments, their municipalities' grants from the federal government must be cut. After all, a large portion of city and state policing funds come from the federal government via grants from the Department of Justice and even the Department of Agriculture. The DOJ's Community Oriented Policing Services program of 1994 has provided $14 billion to salaries and training for local police. If local governments (mostly those of sanctuary cities) are not using this money for the purpose for which it was intended, they should not get it. It is simple in both concept and legality.

Meanwhile, if crime continues to rise over a set threshold, as it very predictably will, these areas should be treated as domestic warzones. This will allow the federal government to take reactive and proactive steps necessary to reduce violence and crime, and to liberate the good people who are hiding in fear within these areas. Portland, during its violent riots and looting, for example, should have been declared a domestic warzone. Those people weren't protesting, but rather celebrating anarchy and destroying property and lives out of pure spite. There's a discernible and codifiable difference.

Next, we must consider that FTO leaders—at least some of them—are not only gold-plated gun-wielding enemies who operate by violence; many are savvy businessmen who operate within the law when they need to. With the amount of money they have, hiring teams of attorneys and paying for top-rate legal counsel is just a cost of doing business. And many have figured out how to use our legal system against itself. They know that their operators and affiliates can claim harassment or racial profiling when they are caught crossing the border. They know that they can send minors to do their bidding whenever possible, and they know that if they wind up in court, they can bleed our system as much as possible throughout the entire lengthy process.

In response, we must pass a law that bans state and local governments from using taxpayer money to defend illegal immigrants in court. The United States has no legal obligation to provide counsel to criminal aliens.

Recently, in early 2023, California Democratic Assemblyman Reggie Jones-Sawyer proposed a bill to fund the legal bills of illegal immigrants, including those who have been convicted of felonies. This should come as no surprise, coming from a state that makes U.S. citizens foot the bill for healthcare and even pandemic relief checks for illegal immigrants. But you may be flabbergasted to learn that the U.S. government paid out $66 million for the legal defense of illegal immigrants facing deportation, according to the Immigration Reform Law Institute (IRLI). With another 1.6 million cases pending, expect $66 million to soon sound like pocket change.[1] The IRLI reports that almost half of the local jurisdictions from across the country that received this money were working closely with the radically progressive nongovernmental organization (NGO) called the Vera Institute of Justice.

If this policy isn't anti-American to its core, as well as criminal, I'm not sure what is. Here we have illegal *criminal* aliens who entered the country illegally, only to surface in America's legal system because they committed crimes—some of them heinous felonies. If they weren't vetted before, they *are* vetted after court! Yet, Americans are unwittingly made to foot the bill for their defense—for defending them against being deported. Yes, law-abiding American citizens are *paying* for criminal aliens to *stay* in America! Due to a mainstream media that is effectively a propaganda wing of any Democrat-controlled White House, very few Americans even know this. Rest assured, it's true. It's happening right now, and it's time Americans say "Enough is enough" by demanding that our leaders reverse this destructive policy.

Most Americans do not believe illegal immigrants—those who broke the law to enter America—much less, those who broke the law *while* here illegally, should be entitled to any special treatment that is supposed to be reserved for U.S. citizens. This is America, so of course every human should be treated humanely, but not every human deserves all the rights that American citizens have. If they desire these unique American rights, there is a legal process in place by which they can obtain citizenship and all the benefits that go with it. American must pass laws barring special treatment of illegal immigrants, including taxpayer-funded care, legal counsel, schooling, housing, and voting rights.

Finally, we also need reform of NGOs in the form of enhanced transparency and accountability so that our own government officials do not become corrupted by them. There are approximately 1.5 million NGOs active in the United States, and there is no law against foreign founding or funding of them. Many are tax exempt. As it stands now, NGOs can influence politicians by giving large donations to their campaigns. Once the politician is beholden to the NGO's demands, it can act like a money-laundering organization, because the government can give the NGO cash in the form of grants, and then the NGO can fund its causes without the government entity having to report it exactly as it would if the money were handed out by the government directly.

There are well-funded NGOs in America right now—both domestically operated and foreign—whose goals are to systematically transform our country into something unrecognizable from what it was intended to be by the Founders and the Constitution. At the very least, NGOs need to be held to the same accountability and transparency standards as the government so the people can see where their tax dollars are going and decide whether they agree with that specific NGO's cause.

These are my basic keys to plugging the holes in our castle and turning the tide in the battle for America's soul. But to be successful in any of this, Americans must use their number one power: the power of the vote. If we are to win this war, we must vote decisively pro-America at the ballot boxes at every opportunity.

What does "pro-America" mean? It means that if you do not like the direction the country is headed in; if you do not like paying for criminal aliens' bills so they can stay in our country while you are struggling to pay your own grocery bill; if you do not like worrying about your son or daughter being exposed to fentanyl; if you do not like the thought of a terrorist blowing up a building or subway just because they do not like America; then you should vote out of office the leaders who do little or nothing to stop these things. Instead, vote into office leaders whose records show they will uphold their oath of office to do all in their power to ensure the safety of citizens. And if these leaders don't hold to their word in the form of immediate, decisive action, we should vote their asses out of office at our first chance.

CHAPTER ELEVEN

The Plan to Save America

Our American heritage is threatened as much by our own indifference as it is by the most unscrupulous office seeker or by the most powerful foreign threat. The future of this Republic is in the hands of the American voter.

—Dwight Eisenhower during a speech to the New York Herald Tribune Forum, New York, New York, October 25, 1949

Now that the floodgates are open, it's easy to *think* that new leadership could instantly secure the border, just as it's easy for candidates to *say* it. While I believe it's doable, because America's political state it won't be easy. But it could be both doable and easy.

The first thing any new administration must have, of course, is the political will—demand from the American people—which I believe a new administration, Democrat or Republican, will have because of the absolute calamity we've witnessed throughout Biden's term. Sure, polls can be wrong, but as of late 2023, polling data suggests Americans are displeased with our current immigration policies.

During my travels all over the country while giving talks on security and running my company that secures large venues, I get the opportunity to converse with many folks from all corners of America. From what I'm hearing in person, I believe border security and immigration will be deciding factors in the 2024 elections. It is *that* important to most of the American people because we know it is *that* important to the sustainability of our nation. Radicals are in for a surprise if they think most Americans want open borders.

I can't help but recall back in mid-September 2023, on national television during a press event held by Democratic New York Representative Alexandria Ocasio-Cortez on her home turf, when those watching witnessed something the outspoken radical congresswoman surely had not anticipated: She was shouted down by event gatherers—her own constituents—who insisted her open border ideologies were disastrous to New Yorkers and who demanded increased border security.

Although Ocasio-Cortez later tried to spin the ordeal by suggesting the event disruptors were conservative plants, subsequent interviews by news media indicated they were not. They were concerned citizens who are fearful of their futures and those of their children. They had reached a boiling point. Some of the most vocal were New York City–based *legal* immigrants who had paid their dues to live in what was once the most iconic city in the world.

Under Ocasio-Cortez's leadership, hotels are full of immigrants and costing city taxpayers $1.35 billion per year to pay for their stays; NYC's total bill for illegal immigrants will be around

$7 billion, which is more than the full budgets of six states! Residents going about their daily lives can't even get down the sidewalks in some areas due to homeless immigrants sleeping on them, with nowhere to go and nothing to do as they pathetically wait for the government to provide. In late September 2023, some New York citizens were arrested as they protested the arrival of yet another bus full of immigrants. By most metrics, including the city's liberal mayor Adams' budget numbers, the city is tanking. In essence, many of Ocasio-Cortez's constituents feel that she is out of touch on this issue. I take this as a good sign for NYC's future.

I believe that all but the most extreme anti-American radicals and special interest groups are turning against open-border policies with each passing day. The situation in several sanctuary cities is simply becoming untenable, not just in New York, and it's spreading everywhere. Meanwhile, the rest of the world is shaking their heads in disbelief as America the beautiful is crumbling under its own hand.

Yet, as worried as I am, I remain optimistic, because I know the following to be true: When Americans rally together in defense of our common homeland, our families, our countrymen, our values, and our freedom, history has proven there is little America cannot do. We saved the world in the early 1940s. You'd better believe we can stem the tide at our own border. But to do so, we'll need people to stand up to the radicals and say, "Enough is enough!" Quite simply, we *must* have a mandate at the polls in 2024.

Once politicians find the political will to tackle this full-blown national security crisis, we must demand they stay the course until it's done, no matter how loud the progressive media moans and plasters images of "kids in cages" all over the nightly news in order to maintain power. "Kids in cages" was a sham concocted by the liberal media, and they know it.

After mustering the political will, the first order of business for a new administration is what Texas Governor Abbott did on September, 22, 2023, when he invoked Article IV, Section 4, and Article I, Section 10 of the U.S. Constitution, which states:

> *The United States shall guarantee to every State in this Union a Republican Form of Government, and shall protect each of them against Invasion; and on Application of the Legislature, or of the Executive (when the Legislature cannot be convened) against domestic Violence.*

Abbott officially called the illegal crossing of 10,000 or more immigrants daily an invasion . . . because it is. He then deployed Texas National Guard and Department of Public Safety troops to Eagle Pass, Texas, and other places to repair the holes in the fence that had been ripped open by Biden-directed operatives and to stand guard against the invasion. In the weeks that followed, Arkansas and Tennessee sent some National Guard troops to assist Texas troops at the border. (At the time of this writing, things are getting dicey between state National Guard troops and the federally deployed troops in that the Border Patrol is being ordered by the Biden administration to take down fencing erected by Texas National Guard troops.)

The point is that once the Constitution is invoked by labeling the mass illegal migration an invasion, thereby mandating the federal government to protect the states from said invasion, many tools in the government's chest can be appropriated to quell it. The next president, Congress, and state governors must invoke it immediately.

Second, and what the Biden administration has never had, is a clear and comprehensive plan.

An effective plan must secure the border immediately, using all emergency means necessary. It must overhaul immigration policy as quickly as possible by passing comprehensive legislation, figure out a way to handle the millions of illegal immigrants already here (I may suggest voluntary military service as one possibility for a fast track to citizenship), and develop sustainable (nonemergency) border security into the future. The plan would also include strengthening domestic employment laws, defunding sanctuary cities, and enforcing the law already on the books concerning illegal aliens.

For starters, we must bring back a honed version of the Secure Communities program that Biden terminated in January 2021. Secure Communities was a data-sharing program between law enforcement and DHS that aggressively pursued criminal aliens. It was designed to record and check the status of each alien who is arrested in the United States, using an instant, sharable biometric database called the Automated Biometric Identification System (IDENT). If an illegal alien surfaces on any government criminal radar, he or she will be identified more quickly than you can sing the national anthem and then deported.

Next, we must erect physical barriers.

Sure, there are elements to physical barriers that are largely symbolic, but hear me out.

Texas set the correct tone in mid-2023 when it stretched floating barriers across popular portions of the Rio Grande. Of course, its detractors say the floating daisy chain of polymer spheres is inhumane and could cause people to drown, but the reality is, a person will not drown if they don't try to cross the border illegally by swimming across the treacherous waters. *Inviting* immigrants to swim across *en masse* results in a net higher loss of life than any barriers.

Likewise, you may or may not know that the millions of immigrants traveling overland from South and Central America must traverse one of the most dangerous and lawless places on Earth—thanks to roving bands of marauders, cartels, and the unforgiving jungle itself—and that is the Darien Gap on the border of Colombia and Panama. Accurate data is, of course, hard to come by in this modern-day Wild West, but plenty of the estimated 400,000 poor immigrants who enter the Darien will never make it out. Many of the casualties are the weakest of the large groups, such as kids, women, and the elderly. Rape, torture, and extortion for safe passage are the norm.

If progressives truly cared about human life as much as they cared about ideologies, they would insist on policies and messaging that discourages these poor people from risking their lives each day. Barriers help send that message in words the entire world can comprehend.

One of the most controversial barriers ever conceived—perhaps rivaling the Berlin Wall in terms of hysterical news fervor, was, of course, Trump's border wall plan that he announced while campaigning for president. Had it not been Trump who initiated it, it might have been built by now with bipartisan approval—who knows? While it's likely that a portion of Trump's purpose for the wall was a symbolic rallying cry for his base, the fact remains: Such a border wall couldn't hurt. It draws a tangible line in the sand that says, *America will protect itself.*

Walls and fences, just like those around your house, your property, or our children's playgrounds, issue a clear ultimatum to any person who doesn't belong inside but who might try to enter. Forcing such an ultimatum is a great way to reveal intent. Either the person can scale the wall, thereby announcing through their action that they are prepared to suffer the consequences if they get caught trespassing, or they can decide that the risk of trespassing isn't worth the effort. At the very least, an obvious physical boundary removes the ability of illegal crossers to claim ignorance of any border they might have crossed, as cartel members routinely do when they are caught sneaking over. (If you believe the two-armed *hombres* that I wrote of earlier were lost as they claimed to Border Patrol, I've got some ocean-front property in Sonora I'll sell you.)

In many state and local jurisdictions in America, law abiding citizens enjoy what is known as the castle doctrine. This law says that anyone who invades the walls of your house (your castle) uninvited can be assumed to have bad intentions. Therefore, it places the burden on the trespassing criminal to prove his or her innocence if they are shot or otherwise attacked by the homeowner who acted in self-defense. Without walls of a house, there would be no clear indicator of how far is too far into someone's intimate place of refuge. Concerning the effectiveness of the castle doctrine, criminals have received the message over time—in fact, most are born with it—and, as prison interviews substantiate, they know they are risking their lives if they breach a homeowner's walls. The result is fewer home invasions in places that have enacted the castle doctrine. We need similar symbolism, security, laws, and universally understood messaging on our border, right now.

Of course, I'm not suggesting we encourage lawless vigilantism that allows citizens to shoot or kill anyone who crosses over a border wall onto American soil on sight—unless innocent lives are in imminent danger, say, if a border-crosser jumps across the border and carjacks someone at gunpoint—but you get the point. A border wall or substantial fence—any obvious barrier denoting a line in the sand—is a universal language that lets people know they will become trespassers and subject to stiff penalties as soon as they cross it. Put plainly, formidable barriers decrease a country's attractiveness. A moat is the opposite of a welcome mat. We must line our border with proverbial razor wire. We need a border wall now, and not just at our southern border, but at our northern border too.

Some left-wing pundits and pro-immigration hawks endlessly bemoan a giant border wall's giant cost. But at an estimated $12 billion, it will be a bargain in the long run if it discourages a couple million illegals from crossing the border over time, not to mention the health costs of unmitigated fentanyl smuggling and acts of terrorism that could possibly be slowed or even thwarted. After all, what's our goal here? To make the cartels' business ventures easier or harder? With some of the policies right now, it's easy to wonder.

I'd also remind these "budget hawks" that the current administration just approved $6 billion to Iraq for a shady prisoner swap, and simply abandoned an estimated $85 billion worth of useful equipment in Afghanistan. Hell, we gave billionaire rapper Kanye "Yeezy" West several million dollars for "COVID relief" so he could continue his rapping. I don't want to hear about wasteful spending—especially not when our national security is at stake.

Fourth, and this is a biggie that would instantly and dramatically help the situation tomorrow if it were enacted: We must allow our Border Patrol, ICE and CBP agents, deportation officials, and law enforcement officers to do their jobs!

In September of 2023, a video captured by Fox News showed an alleged illegal alien getting out of a government-provided bus in San Diego and asking a nearby Border Patrol agent, "It's no problem if I go to Chicago?" To which the BP agent replied, "You can do whatever you want. You're free."

It's safe to assume the individual agent did not make up this policy or decide on the spot that this individual was free. He had been commanded to say it by an unofficial policy and edict passed down from above.

Most of the country's ICE and Border Patrol agents signed up for the job to keep America safe, so I can only imagine what type of stress they are under when they are forced to disobey the oath they took as they perform the duties of a government-paid immigrant concierge service. Indeed, like the police officers that have been defanged and defunded, they are quitting at an alarming rate. These officers wear guns, badges, radios, bullet-proof vests, and handcuffs for a reason, and it's not to direct foot traffic, gather trash, hand out bottled water, and hold the wire of the fence up as an illegal border-crosser crawls under it so it won't scratch his back. These people are trained and equipped to defend the country against foreign invasion, and they are not being allowed to do their jobs. This treasonous directive must be immediately reversed.

Similarly, America has over 200,000 active-duty troops from all branches of the military stationed in dozens of countries. Twenty thousand of them sure would be handy to have overseeing the border right now; you know, helping defend our homeland instead of somebody else's. We could secure the border in a week if our leaders wanted to.

In addition to active troops, there are tens of thousands of combat veterans previously on active duty in the Middle East. Plenty of these salty military men are looking for work similar to what they've been trained for, and they happen to fit the job description of border patrol and cartel assault team perfectly. If the next president is serious about defending the border and sticking taking it to the FTOs—all while providing jobs for trusted, trained, and proven veterans—he or she will initiate a border security and cartel-combating program designed for these patriots as quickly as we could get them there.

There's another group of people who will diligently stand guard near the border if the situation gets any more dire . . . and if they are allowed to. Concerned citizens could be called on to form border and township defense militias if they were given some training and some reasonable protections against liabilities for defending the homeland.

It appears to me that many city dwellers in this country are convinced that the only people who can responsibly carry guns and administer security watches are law enforcement and military personnel. History has proven that this is a fallacy. Texas, Arizona, New Mexico, and yes, even California boast thousands of citizens who would and could provide a line of first defense against illegal border crossings and nefarious behavior in their communities. If our government were so inclined, it could establish an open channel of communication between Border Patrol and law-abiding citizens to keep watch.

It's sad that some people laugh at this notion in today's sue-happy age, but the reality is, few groups of people are in closer proximity to the border, know the country, and are better prepared to report illegal activity than citizens who live there. You can bet your bottom dollar that nefarious border-jumpers are more concerned with armed Texans, Arizonans, and New Mexicans than they are with our Border Patrol under the tutelage of this administration. (To tell you the truth, I'm surprised some angry Texans haven't risen up in defense of their Lone Star state's border already.)

If China's, Russia's, Cuba's, or any other adversarial nation's military invaded our country by way of any U.S. border, I believe armed citizens would answer the call if, when, and where our military somehow struggled to repel the attack on its own. Of course, the Left scoffs at the notion of armed citizens doing anything productive (Who do they think makes up the military?), but we must remember that few on the progressive left even know how to *load* a gun, much less understand its usefulness to citizens bent on defending what's theirs.

We should never unilaterally rule out the possibility of armed and/or deputized American citizens defending their beloved country from overt invasion. The trouble is if politicians are hesitant to define the current invasion as an overt one—and if they ever reach the point of doing so—it would likely be too late. Most of these patriots would proudly bring their own radios, binoculars, and arms for self-defense—and volunteer for this duty for free.

And that brings me to my next step in the plan: how to pay for it.

BUDGETING

You may remember March 22, 2022, when announcing the U.S. 2023 budget, President Biden said, "Don't tell me what you value. Show me your budget, and I'll tell you what you value." And he's right. (See there? I gave the man some credit!)

For 2024, Congress approved $60.4 billion in discretionary spending for DHS programs such as Customs and Border protection, Immigration and Customs Enforcement, Citizenship, and Immigration Services, and many more. Sixty billion dollars sounds like a lot of dough, and it is . . . until it's compared to what we've sent Ukraine for defending itself. Not only does our DHS budget need to be increased at least to the level of what we are giving Ukraine, but the discretionary monies within need to be spent differently, because clearly what the Biden administration is doing with it is not working. For example, new agents need to be hired and trained in a law-enforcement capacity to defend the border from illegal breaches—not hired and trained to make sure illegal immigrants are pampered as they enter.

Here are a few lines from the DHS official Fiscal Year 2024 budget, copied and pasted verbatim as indicated by italics, followed by my comments about them, which are preceded by asterisks.

The FY 2024 President's Budget provides $60.4B in discretionary funding for DHS.

*We wouldn't need nearly that much funding if so much of the money weren't used on programs and staff that encourage illegal immigration rather than repelling it.

Supporting a Fair, Orderly, and Humane Immigration System

*This subhead line would be better for America if it read: "Supporting an Immigration System that puts Americans and America's Security first."

The Nation is enhanced by the millions of immigrants in its industries, businesses, and communities. DHS supports a humane and efficient immigration system that welcomes immigrants and reflects the Nation's values while also enforcing immigration laws.

*It's convenient how the administration omits the word "legal" each time it speaks of immigrants. Most Americans support *legal* immigration. But we do not, and should not, welcome *illegal* immigrants.

To support efficient processing for asylum claimants arriving at the Nation's border, the Budget includes $342M and 1,415 FTE for United States Citizenship and Immigration Services (USCIS) for asylum adjudications; as well as $137M and 612 FTE to fully support the USCIS' International and Refugee Affairs Division, a partner in the U.S. Refugee Admissions Program.

*This is money that is being spent for the mass-processing of illegal immigrants, while it *should* be spent for the deportation of illegal immigrants and the detailed vetting of potential legal immigrants.

The Budget provides $264M and 795 FTE for continued support for the multiyear effort to reduce the application and petition backlog.

*By "reducing the backlog," what the administration sneakily means is that it will rely on the ridiculous CBP One app to shuffle in as many illegal immigrants as possible in the shortest amount of time with no way to account for them later. But, hey, at least they'll clear the backlog so they can wash their hands of any potential "kids in cages" situations.

The Budget includes $84M for the Shelter and Services Program (SSP), which provides funding to support sheltering and related activities provided by non-Federal entities to support U.S. Customs and Border Protection (CBP) in effectively managing noncitizen processing and preventing the overcrowding of short-term CBP holding facilities at the Southwest border.

*This paragraph is also known as the "Illegal Immigrant Concierge Service," which justifies funneling money to NGOs so they can covertly spend taxpayer dollars on plane rides, hotels, cell phones, food, and comforts for illegals so they can enjoy their permanent stay.

The FY 2024 Budget supports the missions of CBP and ICE, including through the following initiatives: The Budget provides $2.5B for ICE Homeland Security Investigations (HSI). HSI is the Department's principal investigative arm and a vital national asset in the global fight against transnational criminal threats. This increase in funding

THE PLAN TO SAVE AMERICA   193

*supports additional personnel and technology enhancements
for investigative capabilities, including $40M for countering
fentanyl and human smuggling and an additional $17M for
child exploitation investigations.*

*So, do your job by letting ICE and CBP agents do theirs.

*The Budget funds $430M for ICE's Transportation and
Removal program. Funding will be used for air charter
flights, commercial flights, and ground transportation
contracts needed to perform necessary removals and costs
associated with increased and expedited travel document
issuance capabilities.*

*Good thinking! Another $430 million of taxpayer
money stuffed in the budget to fly (including with private
jets) and bus illegal immigrants around the United States.
Comfortably. So far, 99 percent of immigrants aren't being
removed, so obviously most of it is going for transportation
elsewhere in the United States.

*The Budget supports $363M for the Alternatives to
Detention (ATD) program, which monitors compliance of
noncitizen participants released pending the outcome of their
immigration proceedings.*

*Another name for this is the "border-hopper honor
system," wherein, provided an illegal alien pinky swears
to show up for a court hearing years down the road, he is
free to go wherever he wants, to do whatever he pleases. It's
insane.

The Budget provides $332M and 283 FTE to support the drawdown of the Department of Defense (DoD) capabilities along the Southwest border.

*Seems like we need a draw*up* of the DoD along the southwest border to most experts, or at least those who have America's best interests in mind.

Additional personnel funded to address the loss of resources from DoD Drawdown includes the hiring of 100 new Border Patrol Agents (BPAs) ($30M), 175 Border Patrol Processing Coordinators (BPPCs) ($15M), 244 Border Patrol Mission Support Staff ($39M), and 46 Office of Field Operations Mission & Operational Support Staff ($7M).

*We need 20,000 additional officers or more, not a few hundred. How about we reappropriate the money spent on thousands of new IRS agents (and guns for them) to more CBP officers instead?

The Budget supports $77M and 330 FTE to recruit/hire additional personnel and ensure applicant suitability in support of Border Management requirements.

*I'm not sure what this means, but knowing this administration, it probably means that a percentage of all Border Patrol agents must be trans, lesbian, or whatever the radical Left deems most suitable to meet its diversity requirements *du jour.*

The Budget funds an increase of $60M for off-site medical expenses of noncitizens in custody, to accommodate the increasing costs of medical care.

*Crossing the river at night under the command of the cartels can certainly be dangerous. Although many American citizens don't have good healthcare, rest assured, illegals will.

Resources in the Contingency Fund will be limited to surge-related functions, undertaken by CBP, ICE, and the Federal Emergency Management Administration (FEMA). Eligible uses for the fund include soft-sided facilities, transportation, detention beds, Alternatives to Detention, and Shelter and Services Program grants to organizations caring for noncitizens, adults and families released from DHS custody.

*I hope those beds are comfy. After all, we are paying for them.

Beds are a nice gesture, but do you know what keeps immigrants out of them in our country? Preventing them from entering in the first place. That's why most of DHS' budget should go to preventive security measures like added technology and equipment for our officers. They should already have it.

Although I hate to bring it up again, I will, because it still sticks in my craw: Remember the estimated $85 to $115 billion worth of equipment Biden and Co. left in Afghanistan during the withdrawal debacle? Much of it, especially the cutting-edge drones, aircraft, 75,000 vehicles, helicopters, biometric equipment, surveillance technology, computer systems, communications systems, body armor, night vision equipment, building supplies, and earth-moving implements would have been extremely useful right now.

Furthermore, we are sending billions upon billions of dollars' worth of such equipment to Ukraine for its defense. We will be sending more for Israel's defense soon. I'd hope we could appropriate a very large portion of our war chest to go to our own.

THE NEXT ADMINISTRATION

The next administration has a choice: It can ask Congress to approve similar DHS budget numbers but reappropriate funds to programs that have proven to be effective against illegal immigration while nixing the entitlement programs for illegal migrants and NGO pork that do little but encourage more illegal immigration, or it can continue our current path of making taxpayers fund the way for illegal immigration and the risks it brings to our national security. I strongly believe the former is the correct path for America. But we, as a people, must demand it.

In short, we must pass H.R. 2 "Secure the Border Act," because it addresses all the steps I've mentioned and much more. In a nutshell, it more clearly defines asylum and refugee claims so that anyone from anywhere can't simply claim asylum to enter America without being an actual refugee from political persecution. It funds completion of the border wall and installs other physical barriers. It mandates the investment in, and installation of, enhanced technology and increased manpower for border security; it mandates the use of an electronic employee-verification system before U.S. employers can hire immigrants; it better equips Border Patrol agents, prohibits DHS from processing illegals who did not enter at an official point of entry, and limits the use of the CBP One app; it installs penalties for visa overstays; it clarifies the procedures for unaccompanied minors; and it mandates accurate reporting of immigrants and myriad other steps of which there are too many to list here. Rest assured, H.R. 2 is great for America and bad for cartels and terrorists. While I'd still advocate for putting more diplomatic and economic pressure on Mexico as well as mobilizing the military against the cartels in case we need it, H.R. 2 is a very good start.

At the time of this writing, the bill has passed the Republican-controlled house. Sadly, there is little chance of it passing the Democrat-controlled Senate until the balance of power changes . . . or until more Democrats realize what is going on and stray from the current party line that encourages open borders. Significantly, H.R. 2 mandates that we establish a clear and thorough plan to secure the border.

Sure, carrying out the plan will be difficult, but it begins with drastic changes in policy, followed by crystal-clear messaging from our government to would-be immigrants and to our officers on the border. We must also send unambiguous messaging in the forms of physical barriers, unwavering law enforcement, and anti-smuggling technology that boldly announces, "You might try to enter illegally, but it won't be easy, and if we catch you, you'll wish you hadn't tried."

Finally, the administration must appoint a border security leader who's an expert on large-scale security and tactics rather than a career politician whose only qualifications for the job include graduating from an Ivy League school and being spineless enough to avoid angering any politician of power.

Yet, none of the outlined plan can or will happen until there is a grassroots effort to elect pro-border security leaders in all of government—from state and local assemblies to Congress and the president.

What is for certain is that while Americans are debating everything from environmental initiatives to abortion, health-care, welfare, trans rights, and college tuition cancellations, millions more noncitizens, including terrorists, will continue to invade our Republic.

It's time to act.

CHAPTER TWELVE

Don't Count America Out

There are leaders out there who still believe in the rule of law. We must elect them now.

—Charles Marino, October 20, 2023

September 9, 2025. Two Miles South of Lajitas, Texas.
The Chihuahuan desert night was clear and cool as the coyote known as *El Sombre*—The Shadow—led three VIP clients out of a natural bunker formed by the rocks where they'd hidden from noon till nightfall. He led them across a dry *arroyo* and around the next hillside, not over it, so they wouldn't be silhouetted by the moonlight as they stopped briefly to make sure all was clear.

The Juarez cartel's top coyote, *Sombre* carried a Chinese-made AK-47 slung across his back that seemed to make his guests happy by the way they admired it. But he rarely used it. The most useful tools in his satchel were a thermal monocular, an encrypted two-way radio, and, mainly, his deep knowledge of the countryside that can only be acquired by a lifetime of living in it.

After 20 minutes of keen surveillance, he whispered a one-word message softly into his radio and then motioned for the three Yemeni nationals to follow him closely, gesturing to stay low, and to move only when he moved. He couldn't help but wonder exactly what these men would do once they reached America, but the nature of their business wasn't discussed. He secretly hoped whatever they carried in those hard-sided backpacks wouldn't be unleashed on El Paso, because he had family there, but he pushed his curiosity out of his mind like the professional that he was. These men were paying his employer $500,000. Not carrying out his orders wasn't an option.

As he took a few steps down the cholla-covered hillside, however, he sensed something strange, a subtle vibration or something, deep in his chest. Instinctively, he shoved his clients down in the tall grass behind a cactus and crouched stone-still as he listened.

In a blur of deafening chops and savage winds, an assault helicopter—a Bell V-280 Valor—materialized over the southern horizon and simultaneously flashed on its blinding spotlights, freezing the four border-hoppers like deer in a poacher's jacklight.

"*Sueltas tu armas! Sueltas tu armas!* Drop your weapons!" they heard from above, as if it were the voice of Allah. But it wasn't Allah . . . or even *El Diablo*. It was worse. *Americans.*

Temporarily blinded, completely surprised, and with nowhere to hide, all four men had enough battle experience to know better than to run. They raised their hands in surrender as a team of eight contracted Special Forces operators fast roped from the hovering craft and deftly surrounded them, carbines shouldered and ready, their eyes glowing a nightmarish green from the NODs attached to their helmets. In mere seconds, the men were apprehended, hands zip-tied, separated, and searched as other members of the team fanned out to secure a perimeter. Ten minutes later, a multinational ground unit arrived on foot to escort them across the border, where they'd be interrogated before being extradited to the one place they most feared: America's penal system.

One glance into the confiscated backpacks confirmed what the assault team's captain had been sent for. They had the right guys, and the shocking intelligence had been dead-on. By working with INTERPOL, Mexico's freshly reformed National Intelligence Centre, and CIA operatives within the Jaurez cartel's network, U.S. intelligence analysts had tracked the jihadi trio overland as they made the one-way journey north from Guatemala and crossed into Mexico before uniting with their hired cartel chaperons.

The Southern Border Terrorist Task Force had just prevented three dirty bombs—radioactive material combined with plastic explosives—from crossing the border into the U.S. homeland. Without a doubt, the terrorists had planned to create lasting destruction, death, chaos, and carnage like never seen before on U.S. soil—on the 24th anniversary of 9/11. But thanks to new policies and an aggressive strategy of cartel counterinsurgency, they were unsuccessful.

While the event I've just described is fiction, it doesn't require a colorful imagination to envision such an evil plot being set in motion right now by terrorists who have exploited our immigration policies. Even the DHS admitted as much in its freshly released 2024 "Homeland Threat Assessment" report. What's more, likely thousands of refugees from Palestine will be granted hasty temporary asylum after the October 2023,

Hamas/Israel conflict, and one can only guess how many terrorists will slip in with them.

The only hope I can offer is, intelligence-based countermeasures such as those I described could be a reality soon—if we make drastic changes in policy now.

But before I get to my suggested plan of action for securing our border, let's take a minute to discuss the root causes that have allowed America's national security to reach such an alarmingly low level. This, after all, is the question Americans most often ask me.

MOTIVES FOR AMERICA'S DEMISE

Dear reader, I talk to you soberly now not to promote my personal brand of politics or any one party. As a security professional trusted by high-profile clients and major news outlets, my intention here is but one: to make America as safe for its citizens as it can possibly be. I try to call it like I see it through an unbiased lens.

Most issues can be settled after thorough debate and compromise among reasonable Americans, or if not, by moving to another area where one's values are better represented. That's the beauty of America. But not this issue. Mass illegal immigration negatively affects us all.

As a security expert formerly employed by DHS, I wrote this book to warn Americans not that the current administration's immigration and border security might fail, but that it *will* fail. If anyone hasn't noticed, it already has. With a sudden influx of 10 million or more impoverished people in just three years since 2020, the United States has been fundamentally changed—there's no way around it. At the same rate, in 20 years we might not even recognize America in terms of its demographics, its available resources, its economy, its culture, its available living space, and its values.

Inviting 10 million unvetted immigrants (most of which are fighting-age, single males) into the country to live on the taxpayer dole while hoping they appear at a parole hearing is asking for large-scale acts of terrorism. It's inevitable. As I've said countless times on national TV, testifying before Congress, and in these pages, we all know most of these immigrants are hard-working, peaceable people who simply wish to have a small slice of the American Dream for themselves. But camouflaged among the good also come the bad. It's a numbers game, and when millions of unknown people with unknown intentions cross our border unchecked, some will be bad apples of the worst kind.

Terrorists, murderers, and drug and human traffickers are exploiting the United States' "compassionate" policies for their own nefarious gain at this very moment. We know this, because we have caught some of them. Their comrades will continue to exploit America's generous nature if they can. How this administration thinks that any terrorist or criminal bent on American carnage will voluntarily show up for a parole hearing years down the road is astounding. Likely, terrorist suicide bombers will already be dead and martyred before any parole hearing comes around.

Indeed, it is so astounding that the question of *why* must be explored. What is the administration's motive for keeping such disastrous policies in place? It keeps me up at night.

In most instances in our talk-happy culture, and especially among our elected officials, when people have differing opinions or are confused about one's actions, you (or a member of the press) can simply ask them: "Excuse me, sir, but why are you doing that? What's the purpose?"

Typically, the person receiving the question (and especially boastful politicians) are all too eager to tell you about the reasoning behind their genius plan so they can sell you on it, or at least satisfy your question with some type of legitimate-sounding answer. And that is what is so puzzling about this administration's actions—moreover its answers—concerning the border. It will not even acknowledge a problem exists, let alone tell the American public why it is doing what it's doing. Don't they know that they are creating distrust?

By denying what people can see is happening with their own eyes, suspicion is created. The fact is, the Biden administration has never, and likely will never, answer the question of why they are letting millions of people in illegally. So, we are forced to speculate and hypothesize if we are to learn from it.

One common refrain I often hear is "The Left hates America." Well, that's not entirely true, or else leftists probably wouldn't live here, and they probably wouldn't try so hard to change something that they fully hate. More accurately, I think, is that they do not like America as it stands now. Specifically, many do not like its system of capitalism, because they've been influenced by an ideology that insists capitalism is unfair and unjust. Some of these people believe anyone who is not equal to another should be made equal through government intervention. When they learn the government is incapable of magically making all people of equal worth, their only option is to tear down the people who they deem to have a higher value. These people believe socialism is a fairer system, and so they try to sabotage capitalism at every turn. They push for policies that increase welfare within America while having capitalists pay for it, thereby—in their confused minds—creating more "equity" between the poor and the rich. (The ironies in this logic are plentiful; namely, the poor immigrants are fleeing socialist policies that have resulted in nationwide poverty to experience American prosperity made possible by capitalism.)

Through their own words, we know that many of these leftist ideologies believe America was founded on imperialism, slavery, racism, violence, and greed, and therefore it is not redeemable and must be started over from scratch. And it must be reset to their liking.

Furthermore, it sure seems like many of these people do not like the demographic makeup of America, which is mostly white. Every action we've seen on the border would indicate that they are trying to change, or at least significantly dilute, America's core demographic makeup over time. Even if they're not purposely trying to alter it, it sure appears that way, judging by the effect.

Perhaps, and much less sinister in intent, some old-school "classical liberals" truly feel that letting everyone in who wishes to enter is the compassionate, humane thing to do. Most of us can understand this sentiment, because we feel for these people, too. The difference is we realize that injecting emotion into national policy rarely ends up creating a better world. It usually results in poor decisions that result in more suffering.

Sure, like the promise of socialism, it's easy to be wooed by the utopian lure of bottomless compassion, but as we discussed earlier in the book, compassion in terms of resources that can be shared has limits, and breaching them can quickly turn compassion into large-scale misery. Some of the open-border advocates naively—often to the point of dangerously—believe that one human race who can all live and work and share together in a globalist utopia is not only possible, but desirable. (I often wonder who, in this Shangri-La land, would get to decide on the form of government and rule of law that everyone must live under, but that's another topic altogether.)

Assuming this administration doesn't outright "hate America," the question then becomes, "Why are they placating a voting base by enacting policies that value immigrants over citizens?"

I've heard very intelligent pundits say it's because the administration is just plain inexperienced—dumb—when it comes to foreign policy. While I don't believe President Biden has his full mental capacity available to him now (I mean this empathetically), his cabinet members certainly do, and they're not dumb. Mayorkas has years of experience in the immigration realm; he knows what he's doing. So, I don't believe this simplistic explanation that's often yelled out of frustration.

One hypothesis is as follows: It's very possible that the administration made a few key blunders early and now feels that it can't correct them, because to do so would be to admit that there is a problem, thereby admitting they made a mistake. Mistakes are bad for poll numbers. Admitting a mistake causes supporters to lose face as well and can influence their future votes.

If this theory is true, it probably started when the administration immediately reversed Trump's Remain in Mexico policy simply because Trump installed it. Perhaps they didn't anticipate that reversing it, together with tearing down Trump's wall, would send a powerful message to immigrants worldwide that America is now open for entry. That's what any reasonable human would think, but especially those who are desperately seeking any opportunity to rush in while they felt their chances of entering might be at a high point.

The next blunder that compounded the problem had already been set in motion by Democrats in Congress and in the media when they blasted the Trump administration in 2018 for detaining illegal immigrants, including families and unaccompanied minors, at the border until these people could be documented and deported back to Mexico or adjudicated as worthy of asylum. This is where the "kids in cages" and "inhumane conditions" anti-Trump media hyperbole came from.

So, when tens of thousands of immigrants began pouring over the border in 2021 thinking they would be welcomed, the Biden administration felt it should not detain them in the same facilities in the same way that its predecessors did, at least not publicly. You may remember about that time, cameras and news teams were banned from taking photos or entering these detention centers. It was only a matter of time before the Biden administration was accused of putting "kids in cages" as well, which was terrible for it politically in the eyes of its base. So, the administration scrambled for some type of scheme that could reduce the numbers of immigrants detained at the border, all while boasting that it would not reinstate any of Trump's policies, which they had blasted for being dumb, cruel, and ineffective only a year earlier. So, what'd they do? They played a shell game; a shell game using human lives.

They modified the CBP One app to publicly appear as a de facto vetting/high-tech processing device so they could disperse immigrants throughout the country (mainly sanctuary cities where the immigrants would be less likely to get arrested and deported) to claim they had fixed the problem on the border. Despite the CBP One app not providing any rock-solid personal data (profile information entered by the user can be fabricated as easily as on a dating app) that they claimed would be used later to find, identify, summon, and vet the millions of immigrants they released into the states, the administration used it to claim that immigrants who used it should not be called *illegal* immigrants, but rather "undocumented" immigrants, or "unverified" immigrants as if it gave them legal standing. (At the time of this writing, the term has been again changed to "irregular immigration" to further soften its sound.)

Of course, this method of digital, expedited entry does not fulfill the requirements mandated by U.S. immigration code; the Left is playing the semantics game like they always do to deceitfully sway public opinion. Why would anyone diligently stand in line for 10 years to get a green card when they could buy a burner phone from a quick stop, create a phony profile, and march across the border into America with several years of immunity and benefits? Such a reckless, preposterous immigration "system" directly undermines America's rule of law while devaluing legal immigration for everyone else. The administration is derelict in the duties entrusted to it.

The administration's next failure was in believing that by making the CBP One app so easy and available to everyone, all immigrants would naturally funnel through official ports of entry. Why would they not? But we soon found out that most immigrants still choose to slip undetected through the fence wherever they can. If they get caught, they can show that they have the app and claim ignorance. If they make it through, there will be no record of them entering, and therefore no chance at vetting. And when such an opportunity exists, you can bet FTOs (cartels) will be ready to exploit it. They are exploiting it right now, getting rich, and laughing.

To that end, the administration underestimated the cartels' technological ability to exploit the app. It was supposed to maintain a geo-fence to filter who could use it to gain entry based on proximity to the border by using cell phone tower location data. But almost instantly, the cartels figured out how to use VPN services to disguise users location data, thereby tricking the geo-fence and enabling them to sell safe passage opportunities to anyone in the world if they came through Mexico. Meanwhile, the Mexican government enacted a policy to allow any non-Mexican immigrant passage through Mexico if they had an American appointment date set, via the app, which anyone and everyone could get. So, hopeful immigrants now come to Mexico from all over the world as a gateway to enter the United States.

As if all these things weren't invitation enough, the Biden administration intentionally or unintentionally put the cherry on top by funneling money to NGOs (and now using FEMA money) to provide flights and bus rides to sanctuary cities, where they would be provided with hotel rooms, food, healthcare, and, for many, work permits. After implementing the app, the administration spun the entire situation by claiming: (1) that there is not a problem on the *border*; (2) that many immigrants are here legally; and (3) that they are providing a necessary new work force to bolster the economy.

They even try to spin the fact that 160 people with ties to terrorism have been caught in the process, by saying, "See? The system works! We caught them!" The trouble is double or triple that number might have not been caught. We don't know and we likely won't . . . until there's another 9/11.

Illegal immigrants are getting the red-carpet welcome message loud and clear, as proven by the fact they keep coming by the millions. And they will keep coming until our policies change.

So, there it is, the "Biden Border Blunder" hypothesis. Yet for as damaging and stupid as it sounds, I hope it's correct, because it troubles me to even contemplate the treasonous other motives that are possible; motives that many citizens think are the true reasons behind this administration's policies. It's entirely possible that their motive is solely for political payoff.

It is very possible that the Democrats are simply using the border crisis (Never waste a good crisis, remember?) and resulting mass immigration movement as a voter-recruitment tool. After all, that play is a common one, and it makes logical sense once the full playing field is studied on a macro level.

In 24 states plus Washington, D.C., the latest of which is Democrat-controlled Pennsylvania, Democrats have enacted laws that automatically register people to vote as they obtain a driver's license. They do not have to be citizens under Pennsylvania law. Allowing foreign nationals to vote in American elections is unconstitutional on its face, yet it's happening to the delight of Democrats in those states.

Meanwhile, what has Joe Biden recently enacted, by executive order, for half a million illegal immigrants from Venezuela, with millions more from such places as Haiti surely to follow? The right to work and to get a driver's license. Thus, millions of technically illegal immigrants will be able to vote. If immigrants don't vote, more registered souls mean more ballots that can be harvested, making voter fraud easier. Some people get angry when the phrase "voter fraud" is uttered—probably because Trump uttered it many times—but you can't tell me that there are zero cases of voter fraud. It happens. We must try to minimize it.

If you think all of these pieces do not fit into a puzzle, you are underestimating the influence that Saul Alinsky has had on these people. The Marxist Saul Alinsky taught his "community organizer" disciples that any means to an end is justified—if it is for a good cause. Of course, the definition of "good" is highly debatable and is most often defined by those in power—even if that power was gained through deceptive means. They are also employing the Cloward-Piven strategy of inducing a shift to socialism by manufacturing a crisis that can then be leveraged to maximize the number of people on welfare so that redistribution of wealth becomes normalized. (They employed this nation-altering strategy during the COVID-19 pandemic.)

More simply, if the administration lets immigrants in and gives them handouts to make them dependent on those in power, they believe most of those immigrants will become loyal Democrat voters. It's sick, and I hope I'm wrong but I don't think I am.

My final hypothesis, and the one that I lean toward believing most, is a combination of all the above.

It's very possible, if not likely, that a series of blunders and lack of foresight by the Biden White House exacerbated the border and immigration problem that had ramped up from the economic collapse of several South American countries. But now that mass migration is happening, Democrats are happy to reap what they consider to be benefits from it, including: changing what they view to be an imperialistic culture that favors white men; promulgating entitlement programs that will set the stage for a more European-style socialist systems in the future; doing their part to fulfill a one-world utopian dream; and mining loyal Democrat voters for future elections.

If you have a theory, I'd love to hear it sometime. In the end, though, it doesn't matter who is installing these destructive policies or why they are doing it. What matters is that the American people recognize that their very security is at stake and that we make the necessary course corrections before it's too late.

WHY MY APPROACH WILL WORK

Physically regaining operational control of our borders is difficult, but it's not impossible. It starts with letting illegal crossers know, in no uncertain terms, that there is no refuge for them here unless their lives are in immediate danger, they have nowhere else to go, and they can prove it. If they are caught crossing illegally, not only will they have risked their lives, only to be turned away, but they will leave with a shiny new criminal record that will prevent them from entering legally in the future. Cartel members will find out that if they are captured, they will be given prison terms long enough to see Halley's Comet passing twice—if only they could see the sky.

Then we must back up this messaging with unwavering commitment to it by way of ample budget, security via manpower and technology, and strict enforcement of our laws.

The plan will work, because it has worked reasonably well here for so many years in the past. I'm not implying, of course, that we'll keep 100 percent of all illegals out—that's impossible. But we can raise the drawbridges. Once immigrants find out they can't enter the United States on a whim, many will likely go back home. If they are truly political refugees of hellhole countries where they could possibly be killed, tortured, or enslaved for their religious or political views, they'll either decide that Mexico is a significant step up, or they will apply for asylum in America and immigrate here legally, by the codified, regulated process that we have established. It will work, because the American people will not accept anything less; our law enforcement officers, and our military, if necessary, will help ensure it. America remains the 800-pound gorilla of the globe. If we need to rattle a few neighbors' cages or cut them off from America's handout spigot for a while, we can.

One big component of my strategy that will make the entire process much easier for us is to gain the cooperation of the Mexican government. Think about it: Without Mexico's earnest support in solving this problem, we can and will go it alone, but it will likely get ugly. In 1994 and again in 2003, we engaged in long, costly wars over the threat of terrorism reaching our shores and those of our allies. The current national security threat made possible in large part by Mexico failing to get a handle on its cartel problem should be treated in the same manner. First, we try diplomacy, then we apply economic pressure, then we play hardball. If none of these works—though I'm confident they will if a competent administration is handling the negotiations—we will destroy the cartels surgically as the good ol' USA can, or at least maim them so badly that they must look over their shoulders in fear for the rest of their scurvy lives.

Once we regain operational control over our borders, we can then begin a national dialogue about comprehensive reform and pathways to citizenship for some of the immigrants already here—those who, after thorough vetting of character, prove themselves capable of being assets to America, not anchors.

I believe history will deem the next administration to be either a meager one that put the last few nails in our great Republic's coffin . . . or the bold one that saved it from history's heap of short-lived superpowers. The latter outcome will not, and cannot, happen without us, free Americans, uniting as a collective force, demanding it publicly, loudly, continuously, and fearlessly. The American people must elect leaders who place America's national security at the very top of the list of its priorities. We must elect a president, senators, and representatives whose *actions* prove that they believe in the oath of office they swore to uphold—leaders who are willing to risk their political futures in exchange for America's.

Epilogue

If our primary concern is national security, then whom should we elect in 2024? While this book was not written to hype specific candidates, if track record is an indicator—which it most certainly is—Americans may find themselves in a rare but fortunate position come November.

Only a few times in U.S. history has a president run for re-election in nonconsecutive terms. In other words, if the race comes down to a rematch of Biden versus Trump, Americans have the advantage of judging both candidates not by what they *say* they will do *if* they are elected president, but rather by what they *did* in four years *as* president.

Donald Trump's policies were clearly better for Americans than Biden's. Trump was bold in his negotiations, just as he was in crafting his immigration and border policies that mandated asylum seekers be throughly vetted before gaining entry. Remain in Mexico was his centerpiece policy, and one that never should have been slashed by the 46th president soon after taking office.

In terms of his commitment to doing what must be done to ensure America's security and preparedness against terrorist attacks and dangerous illegal immigration, Trump is solid.

This we know. If elected in 2024, he says he will begin by enacting mass deportations of illegals. Based on his track record, I believe him.

Fact is, most Democrats do not actually believe America should have open borders. Yet most are very cautious about publicly saying as much to far left factions of their base. They are also generally leery of saying anything that could possibly be construed as sounding like Trump—even if it means taking a soft line on America's security.

By now we all know where President Biden stands on this issue—and more important, what his policies have caused. Despite what he and his spokespeople say, the president's dismal record on America's border security is unparalleled in modern American history. Facts don't lie.

So as you consider for whom to cast your vote, remember this: Believe not what a candidate says, but rather what his or her prior actions portend. If we are to right this incredible ship known as the United States of America, we must vote for candidates who prioritize the security of our country now, before it's too late.

Notes

CHAPTER 1

1. DHS Office of Immigration Statistics.
2. Meet the Press. September 11, 2022 (nbcnews.com).
3. Charles Marino and Katherine Kuhlman. "Biden's Border Problem: A Perfect Storm for National Security and Local Communities." *The Hill*, August 3, 2021
4. Statista.com.
5. CBP Enforcement Statistics fiscal year 2023, U.S. Customs and Border Protection.
6. DHS Office of Homeland Security Statistics.

CHAPTER 2

1. Paul Kupiec. "The Migrant and Housing Crises Are Colliding with Predictable Results." *The Hill*, October 5, 2023.
2. William La Jeunesse. "Most Illegal Immigrants Receive Government Benefits, Costing Taxpayers Billions: Experts." Fox News.
3. Charles Marino. "The Mexican Cartels: Insurgencies or Criminal Organizations?" Paper, National War College, 2012.
4. Joseph Trevino. "Border Agent on Letting in 'Gang Members': 'I Feel Like I'm Part of the Smuggling Organization.'" *New York Post*, October 10, 2023.
5. Jennie Taer. "Feds Flagged Nearly 75,000 Illegal Migrants as Potential National Security Risks." *Daily Caller*, September 1, 2023.
6. CPB.gov official statistics.
7. Pete Williams. "FBI Director Wray Says Scale of Chinese Spying in the U.S. 'Blew Me Away.'" NBC News, February 1, 2022.
8. "How Much Do Drugs Cost: The Steep Price of Addiction." AddictionCenter.com.

9. Jennifer Griffin and Liz Friden. "Gone Too Soon: Fentanyl Flowing from China." Fox News, June 22, 2022.
10. Ibid.

CHAPTER 3

1. Laura Gottesdiener. "A Family Business: How and Why Smugglers Are Bringing More Children to the U.S. Border." *Reuters*, March 23, 2021.
2. Nicole Fallert. "Video Shows Migrants Thanking Joe Biden for Support Before Apprehension at Border." Newsweek.com, March, 25, 2021.
3. "Morning Joe." MSNBC, March 2019.
4. ICE Enforcement and Removal Operations Annual Reports.
5. Simon Hankinson. "Biden Lets in Immigrants and Taxpayers Get Stuck with the Bill." Fox News, July 28, 2023.
6. John Gramlich. "Key Facts about Title 42, the Pandemic Policy that Has Reshaped Immigration Enforcement at United States–Mexico Border." Pew Research Center, April 27, 2022.
7. Interim Staff Report of the Committee on the Judiciary and Subcommittee on Immigration Integrity, Security, and Enforcement U.S. House of Representatives; "The Biden Border Crisis: New Data and Testimony Show How the Biden Administration Opened the Southwest Border and Abandoned Interior Enforcement." October 9, 2023.
8. Mohamad Moslimani. "How Temporary Protected Status Has Expanded Under the Biden Administration." Pew Research Center, April 21, 2023.
9. Adam Shaw and Bill Melugin. "5,000 Illegal Immigrants Released Every Day into US, Admin Officials Privately Tell Lawmakers." Foxnews.com, Dec. 9, 2023.
10. Elizabeth Heckman. "Enraged Border Agents Accuse Biden Admininstration of Sabotaging Operations: Activists 'Taking Over' Law Enforcement." Fox News, May 9, 2023.

CHAPTER 4

1. "Illegal Immigration Now Costs American Taxpayers at Least $151 Billion a Year." FAIRUS.org, March 8, 2023.

CHAPTER 6

1. Fentanyl-Fact-Sheet-23.01.24-v1.pdf. thenationalcouncil.org.

2. "Drug Enforcement Administration Announces the Seizure of Over 379 Million Deadly Doses of Fentanyl in 2022." Drug Enforcement Administration.

CHAPTER 7

1. Andrew Dorn and Steve Joachim. "Interactive Map: Tracking Cartel Arrests Across the Country." NewsNation, February 16, 2023.

CHAPTER 8

1. "Victims of Intentional Homicide." United Nations Office on Drugs and Crime.
2. "United Nations Convention Against Corruption." United Nations Office on Drugs and Crime, 2004.
3. Kendal Blust. "National Survey Shows Prevalence of Police and Public Servant Bribes in Mexico in 2021." Fronterasdesk.org, January 31, 2022.

CHAPTER 10

1. "Over $66 Million in Taxpayer Funds Used to Defend Illegal Aliens in Court." Investigative Reports, February 28, 2023.

Index

About the Author

CHARLES MARINO currently serves as the CEO of a leading global security and intelligence advisory firm.

He is a recognized expert on national security policy, programs, operations, and emerging threats. Charles regularly appears on major cable news networks to provide expert analysis on national security issues impacting the United States and is also an Adjunct Professor at the University of South Carolina Honor College where he teaches a class entitled, "The Politics of National Security."

As a former Supervisory Special Agent in the United States Secret Service and career Senior Law Enforcement Advisor to former DHS Secretary Janet Napolitano, Charles oversaw the creation and implementation of complex homeland security and law enforcement programs like the Southwest Border Law Enforcement Engagement Strategy, the See Something, Say Something national campaign, and the National Terrorism Advisory System (NTAS).

Charles is a 2012 graduate of the National Defense University, National War College, where he earned a Master of Science degree in National Security Strategy.

Most important, Charles is a proud American citizen who will stop at nothing to keep his fellow citizens safe from senseless and often preventable crime.

Visit the author at CharlesMarino.com.